Katherine –
  May the waters you
crossed every day to
come to school connect
you to wondrous waters
of the world and inspire
travels and writing
about those travels.
                    Love,
                      Vicki

June 2008
Congratulations!

DARK WATERS DANCING TO A BREEZE

edited and with an introduction by
WAYNE GRADY

A LITERARY COMPANION
to RIVERS & LAKES

DARK WATERS
DANCING
TO A BREEZE

 David Suzuki Foundation

GREYSTONE BOOKS
DOUGLAS & MCINTYRE PUBLISHING GROUP
VANCOUVER/TORONTO/BERKELEY

07 08 09 10 11   5 4 3 2 1

Greystone Books
A division of Douglas & McIntyre Ltd.
2323 Quebec Street, Suite 201
Vancouver, BC, Canada V5T 4S7
www.greystonebooks.com

David Suzuki Foundation
219–2211 West 4th Avenue
Vancouver, BC, Canada V6K 4S2

Library and Archives Canada Cataloguing in Publication
Dark waters dancing to a breeze : a literary companion to rivers
and lakes / edited and with an introduction by Wayne Grady.
Co-published by the David Suzuki Foundation.

ISBN 978-1-55365-244-1

1. Rivers—Literary collections. 2. Lakes—Literary collections. 3. Water—Literary collections.
I. Grady, Wayne II. David Suzuki Foundation
PN6071.W37D37 2007   808.84'9321693   C2007-900417-2

Cover and text design by Peter Cocking
Cover images © Veer Incorporated
Printed and bound in Canada by Friesens
Printed on acid-free paper that is forest friendly
(100% post-consumer recycled paper) and has been processed chlorine free.
Distributed in the U.S. by Publishers Group West

We gratefully acknowledge the financial support of the Canada Council for the Arts,
the British Columbia Arts Council, and the Government of Canada through the Book
Publishing Industry Development Program (BPIDP) for our publishing activities.

CONTENTS

DARK WATERS DANCING TO A BREEZE

INTRODUCTION

—

WHETHER WE ARE conscious of it or not, water is omnipresent in our lives. This is literally true, since our bodies are 70 percent water and because, for practical as well as other reasons, most towns and cities are built beside water. With a bit of thought, we can section the course of our lives by the rivers or lakes we've lived or traveled on.

I was born on the south—that is, the Canadian—shore of the Detroit River, at a time when that engineered link in the chain of the Great Lakes was little more than a convenience for factory owners and distillers. I grew up fishing the myriad small streams that meander through the pastures of southern Ontario, with a Woolworth's rod and a can of worms. Later I lived on the great, sand-charged Moisie River in northern Quebec and camped in stands of balsam fir and black spruce just where the river hooked into the St. Lawrence, the Moisie's green corridor to my left and the flat, mile-wide, salt expanse of *La Fleuve* on my right. (In French, *fleuve* is both a river and something greater than a river, almost a cultural term, as in a river of tears, or of blood, something that flows out of us.) I've walked beside the Red Deer River where it slid through the Alberta Badlands, thick and warm and sluggish as melted chocolate, and have threaded my way along dry arroyos in northern Patagonia, their sandy banks riddled with swallow nests and their bottoms rippled by long-absent rainwater. I've hiked along the Yukon River, where once, from the top of a high cliff on my way to Dawson City, I peered over the edge as an eagle flew by just below my feet.

The prevalence of rivers and lakes in our lives is not mere happenstance. Evidence from evolutionary psychology suggests that water is a vital element in human nature: it helps define who we are. Studies of various cultures show that, given a choice, most people prefer to live on a height of land overlooking a savanna-like grassland containing a few isolated trees, with a view of a river, a lake, or the sea. E.O. Wilson, in his book *Creation,* cites such studies in support of his contention, which I share, that *Homo sapiens* is a grassland species: we evolved on a subtropical African savanna and feel most secure with a commanding view of the terrain before us containing lots of browsing game and edible plants, and "a body of water nearby [that serves] as a territorial boundary and an added source of food."

In other words, we are hard-wired for water. Rivers and lakes have been flowing through our consciousness since the first *Homo sapiens* scooped a crayfish from a grassland stream and realized it tasted better than euphorbia leaves. The Bible refers to rivers as "the waters of life," and Genesis specifies that "a river flowed out of Eden to water the garden, and there it divided into four rivers": their names were Pison, Gihon, Tigris, and Euphrates. In a land in which most "rivers" are *wadis* that dry up between rains, a true river that runs year-round, whose waters sparkle and dance in the sun and wind, makes paradise seem possible. In the ancient Hako ceremony, which recounts the spiritual history of the Pawnee people of the North American Great Plains, the first thing the ancestors see on their quest for "the land of the Son" are trees growing along the banks of a stream: "We sing to the river, and when we come nearer and see the water and hear it rippling, then we sing to the water." This distinction between the river and the water in it is also found in English: our word "river" comes from the Latin *ripa,* which technically means river *bank*—the land beside, not the water in, a river. Two groups of people living on the same river were called *rivals,* which eventually came to mean opponents, since both groups presumably vied for the same water, or the fish that lived in it, or the trade that came by it. To *derive* means to divert water from a river for irrigation, and to *arrive* means to come ashore after a river crossing.

Rivers (and lakes, which as Rupert Brooke notes, are often little more than swollen rivers, "fresh-water streams that have married and settled down"), are life-giving in a literal as well as a spiritual sense. We can live without food for weeks, but without water we die in four days. Towns situated far from water seldom flourish. Nations with precarious water supplies languish or become fractious, while those with plenty of water prosper. As Michael Specter noted in a recent issue of the *New Yorker*, "most of the world's great civilizations grew up around rivers, and few forces have so clearly shaped the destiny of human populations." He also points out, "the Chinese character for 'political order' is based on the symbol for water."

Of course, any symbol as deeply rooted in our collective imagination as water will be ambiguous, and rivers have been identified with death as well as with life. The goal of a river is, after all, to lose itself in the fathomless sea, just as the soul is supposed to yearn for oneness with the unknowable afterlife. "Let Rome in Tiber melt," declares Shakespeare's Mark Antony to Cleopatra, a sentiment completed by Tennyson in his poem "The Princess": "Let the great river take me to the main..." To follow a river to its logical conclusion, which is oblivion, is therefore the perfect metaphor for life, as we know from *The Adventures of Huckleberry Finn, Apocalypse Now*, and Matthew Arnold:

> A wanderer is man, from his birth.
> He was born in a ship
> On the breast of the river of Time.

The stories in this collection reflect our connection to and fascination with water, especially water on the move. Great literature has the ability to make material that which we feel viscerally, and so whether we stand with Nathaniel Hawthorne in awestruck wonder at the sheer volume of water cascading over Niagara Falls, "haunted with a vision of foam and fury," or contemplate with Bruce Hutchison the power of the upper reaches of British Columbia's Fraser River, "forever mad, ravenous and lonely," we hear the rivers' thunder in our ears and feel the Earth shaking our bones. Northrop Frye has written about the sense of foreboding early immigrants to Canada must have felt as the St. Lawrence River slowly drew them into the belly of the continent, so many Jonahs being swallowed by Leviathan, and we share that same sense when we read Australian novelist Kate Grenville describing an early penetration of the Hawkesbury River, which empties into Broken Bay north of what is now Sydney: "What had seemed a dead end slyly opened up into a stretch of river between cliffs." River writing is essentially sensual; we hear, feel, and respond in subconscious recognition.

When we read about water, in other words, we can feel it, smell it, and taste it, and that may be why so much river writing is about fishing: fish are the living embodiment of water. In fact, fish stories are probably the oldest in human culture. That early *Homo sapiens* sniffing at a crayfish in the Rift Valley, or my ten-year-old self admiring rainbow trout as they darted away from my hook in southern Ontario, were participating in the direct tangibility of water, recognizing water as both a living and an aesthetic experience—which is perhaps what Alaskan nature writer John A. Murray meant when he "reflected on the similarities between fishing and nature writing," or why James Dickey could declare that there's not much to choose between a trout line and a line of poetry. The first book in English about rivers—Izaak Walton's *The Compleat Angler*—is also the first book about fishing. Fish moving below the water's surface without any apparent effort remind us of the way thoughts glide through the brain. In these pages, John Burroughs recognizes the congruity when he writes that "on all the expeditions in which [speckled trout] has been the ostensible purpose I have brought home more game than my creel showed." There is no daily limit on thoughts, but they do lend themselves to catch-and-release, for which we're grateful. In Burroughs's "harmless, preoccupied" fisherman, do we not also see the poet, whose "mind is in the creek" and whose preoccupation "anneals him and makes him pliable to the scenes and influences he moves among"?

Whether we're fishing (Walton, Burroughs, Ted Williams, Norman Maclean) or conveying ourselves over water (Henry Walter Bates, John McPhee, William Least Heat-Moon, Jill Frayne), meditating beside it (Hawthorne, Mark Twain, Donald Culross Peattie), or taking notes (Charles Darwin, Kevin Van Tighem), or simply reading about the life aquatic, we're participating in activities that are as old as humanity itself. There's a reason we want that view of water in front of us, and it is not simply a matter of territoriality or a reliable source of protein: we long to inhabit that magical realm where water, yielding to the pull of the reflected moon, laps the land; a realm in which we can cease our restless wandering; a place where, at last, we can arrive.

CONCERNING RIVERS

IZAAK WALTON

Born in Stafford, England, in 1593, Walton worked as an ironmonger in London, married a grand-niece of Thomas Cranmer, the archbishop of Canterbury, in 1626, and retired to Winchester in 1644 with a sizeable competence. He wrote biographies of the poets John Donne (1640) and Sir Henry Wotton (1651) but is chiefly remembered for his whimsical discourse on the art of fishing, *The Compleat Angler, or The Contemplative Man's Recreation*. First published in 1653, it takes the form of a leisurely debate between Piscator, a fisherman, and Venator, a huntsman, as they fish along the river Lea, near London; Venator is gradually persuaded that fishing is a more congenial pursuit than hunting. In this excerpt, Piscator builds his case by invoking some of the ancient lore and timeless fascination of rivers.

. . .

AN INGENIOUS SPANIARD says, that "rivers and the inhabitants of the watery element were made for wise men to contemplate and fools to pass by without consideration." And though

I will not rank myself in the number of the first, yet give me leave to free myself from the last, by offering to you a short contemplation... concerning rivers: there be so many wonders reported and written of them, and of the several creatures that be bred and live in them; and those by authors of so good credit, that we need not to deny them an historical faith.

As namely of a river in Epirus, that puts out any lighted torch, and kindles any torch that was not lighted. Some waters being drank cause madness, some drunkenness, and some laughter to death. The river Selarus in a few hours turns a rod or wand to stone, and our Camden mentions the like in England, and the like in Lochmere in Ireland. There is also a river in Arabia, of which all the sheep that drink thereof have their wool turned into a vermilion colour. And one of no less credit than Aristotle tells us of a merry river (the river Elusina) that dances at the noise of music, for with music it bubbles, dances, and grows sandy, and so continues till the music ceases, but then it presently returns to its wonted calmness and clearness. And Camden tells us of a well near to Kirby in Westmoreland, that ebbs and flows several times every day: and he tells us of a river in Surrey (it is called Mole), that after it has run several miles, being opposed by hills, finds or makes itself a way under ground, and breaks out again so far off, that the inhabitants thereabouts boast (as the Spaniards do of their river Anus) that they feed divers flocks of sheep upon a bridge. And lastly, for I would not tire your patience, one of no less authority than Josephus, that learned Jew, tells us of a river in Judea that runs swiftly all the six days of the week, and stands still and rests all their sabbath.

A FLOOD

JOHN JAMES AUDUBON

John James Audubon was born Jean Rabin on the island of Santo Domingo (now Haiti) in 1785, the illegitimate son of Lieutenant Jean Audubon and his Creole mistress. He was adopted by Audubon and taken to France, where he studied drawing under the French artist Jacques-Louis David until, at the age of eighteen, he was sent to oversee his father's property at Mill Grove, near Norristown, Pennsylvania. In 1818 he moved to Cincinnati, Ohio, where he supported his family by drawing portraits. His first publication, the monumental *Birds of America*, with 1,065 life-sized portraits of North American birds, was published in London in 1827; the seven-volume American edition followed in 1840–44. Audubon traveled widely for his painting, mostly by river, since that was where the birds were. This account of a flood on the Mississippi and Ohio rivers provides an early and eerily familiar description of the destruction wrought by nature, presaging the 2005 Hurricane Katrina disaster.

. . .

MANY OF OUR LARGER streams, such as the Mississippi, the Ohio, the Illinois, the Arkansas and the Red River, exhibit at certain seasons the most extensive overflowings of their waters, to which the name of *floods* is more appropriate than the term *freshets,* usually applied to the sudden risings of smaller streams. If we consider the vast extent of country through which an inland navigation is afforded by the never-failing supply of water furnished by these wonderful rivers, we cannot suppose them exceeded in magnitude by any other in the known world. It will easily be imagined what a wonderful spectacle must present itself to the eye of the traveller, who for the first time views the enormous mass of waters, collected from the vast central regions of our continent, booming along, turbid and swollen to overflowing, in the broad channels of the Mississippi and Ohio, the latter of which has a course of more than a thousand miles, and the former of several thousands.

To give you some idea of a *booming flood* of these gigantic streams, it is necessary to state the causes which give rise to it. These are, the sudden melting of the snows on the mountains, and heavy rains continued for several weeks. When it happens that, during a severe winter, the Alleghany Mountains have been covered with snow to the depth of several feet, and the accumulated mass has remained unmelted for a length of time, the materials of a flood are thus prepared. It now and then happens that the winter is hurried off by a sudden increase of temperature, when the accumulated snows melt away simultaneously over the whole country, and the south-easterly wind which then usually blows, brings along with it a continued fall of heavy rain, which, mingling with the dissolving snow, deluges the alluvial portions of the western country, filling up the rivulets, ravines, creeks, and small rivers. These, delivering their waters to the great streams, cause the latter not merely to rise to a surprising height, but to overflow their banks, wherever the land is low. On such occasions, the Ohio itself presents a splendid, and at the same time an appalling spectacle; but when its waters mingle with those of the Mississippi, then is the time to view an American flood in all its astonishing magnificence.

At the foot of the Falls of the Ohio, the water has been known to rise upwards of sixty feet above its lowest level. The river, at this point, has already run a course of nearly seven hundred miles, from its origin at Pittsburgh, in Pennsylvania, during which it has received the waters of its numberless tributaries, and overflowing all the bottom lands or valleys, has swept along the fences and dwellings which have been unable to resist its violence. I could relate hundreds of incidents which might prove to you the dreadful effects of such an inundation, and which have been witnessed by thousands besides myself. I have known, for example, of a cow swimming through a window, elevated at least seven feet from the ground, and sixty-two feet above low-water mark. The house was then surrounded by water from the Ohio, which runs in front of it, while the neighbouring country was overflowed; but the family did not remove from it, but remained in its upper portion, having previously taken off the sashes of the lower windows, and opened the doors. But let us return to the Mississippi.

There the overflowing is astonishing; for no sooner has the water reached the upper part of the banks, than it rushes out and overspreads the whole of the neighbouring swamps, presenting an ocean overgrown with stupendous forest-trees. So sudden is the calamity, that every individual, whether man or beast, has to exert his utmost ingenuity to enable him to escape from the dreaded element. The Indian quickly removes to the hills of the interior; the cattle and game swim to the different strips of land that remain uncovered in the midst of the flood, or attempt to force their way through the waters until they perish from fatigue. Along the banks of the river, the inhabitants have rafts ready made, on which they remove themselves, their cattle and their provisions, and which they then fasten with ropes or grape-vines to the larger trees, while they contemplate the melancholy spectacle presented by the current, as it carries off their houses and wood-yards piece by piece. Some who have nothing to lose, and are usually known by the name of *squatters*, take this opportunity of traversing the woods in canoes for the purpose of procuring game, and particularly the skins of animals, such as the deer and bear, which may be converted into money. They resort to the low ridges surrounded by the waters, and destroy thousands of deer, merely for their skins, leaving the flesh to putrefy.

The river itself, rolling its swollen waters along, presents a spectacle of the most imposing nature. Although no large vessel, unless propelled by steam, can now make its way against the current, it is seen covered by boats, laden with produce, which running out from all the smaller streams, float silently towards the City of New Orleans, their owners meanwhile not very well assured of finding a landing-place even there. The water is covered with yellow foam and pumice, the latter having floated from the Rocky Mountains to the north-west. The eddies are larger and more powerful than ever. Here and there tracts of forest are observed undermined, the trees gradually giving way, and falling into the stream. Cattle, horses, bears and deer are seen at times attempting to swim across the impetuous mass of foaming and boiling water; whilst here and there a vulture or an eagle is observed perched on a bloated carcass, tearing it up in pieces, as regardless of the flood as on former occasions it would have been of the numerous *sawyers* and *planters*, with which the surface of the river is covered, when the water is low. Even the steamer is frequently distressed. The numberless trees and logs that float along break its paddles and retard its progress. Besides, it is on such occasions difficult to procure fuel to maintain its fires; and it is only at very distant intervals that a wood-yard can be found which the water has not carried off.

Following the river in your canoe, you reach those parts of the shores that are protected against the overflowing of the waters, and are called *levees*. There you find the whole population of the district at work repairing and augmenting those artificial barriers, which are several feet above the level of the fields. Every person appears to dread the opening of a *crevasse*, by which the waters may rush into his fields. In spite of all exertions, however, the crevasse opens, the water bursts impetuously over the plantations, and lays waste the crops which so lately were blooming in all the luxuriance of spring. It opens up a new channel, which, for aught I know to the contrary, may carry its waters even to the Mexican Gulf.

I have floated on the Mississippi and Ohio when thus swollen, and have in different places visited the submersed lands of the interior, propelling a light canoe by the aid of a paddle. In this manner I have traversed immense portions of the country overflowed by the waters of these rivers, and, particularly whilst floating over the Mississippi bottomlands, I have been struck with awe at the sight. Little or no current is met with, unless when the canoe passes over the bed of a bayou. All is silent and melancholy, unless when the mournful bleating of the hemmed in deer reaches your ear, or the dismal scream of an eagle or a raven is heard, as the foul bird rises, disturbed by your approach, from the carcass on which it was allaying its craving appetite. Bears, cougars, lynxes, and all other quadrupeds that can ascend the trees, are observed crouched among their top branches. Hungry in the midst of abundance, although they see floating around them the animals on which they usually prey, they dare not venture to swim to them. Fatigued by the exertions which they have made in reaching the dry land, they will there stand the hunter's fire, as if to die by a ball were better than to perish amid the waste waters. On occasions like this, all these animals are shot by hundreds.

Opposite the City of Natchez, which stands on a bluff of considerable elevation, the extent of inundated lands is immense, the greater portion of the tract lying between the Mississippi and the Red River, which is more than thirty miles in breadth, being under water. The mail-bag has often been carried through the immersed forests, in a canoe, for even a greater distance, in order to be forwarded to Natchitochez.

But now, observe this great flood gradually subsiding, and again see the mighty changes which it has effected. The waters have now been carried into the distant ocean. The earth is everywhere covered by a deep deposit of muddy loam, which in drying splits into deep and narrow chasms, presenting a reticulated appearance, and from which, as the weather becomes warmer, disagreeable, and at times noxious, exhalations arise, and fill the lower stratum of the atmosphere as with a dense fog. The banks of the river have almost everywhere been broken down in a greater or less degree. Large streams are now found to exist, where none were formerly to be seen, having forced their way in direct lines from the upper parts of the bends. These are by the navigator called *short-cuts*. Some of them have proved large enough to produce a change in the navigation of the Mississippi. If I mistake not, one of these, known by the name of the *Grand Cut-off,* and only a few miles in length, has diverted the river from its natural course, and has shortened it by fifty miles. The upper parts of the islands present a bulwark consisting of an enormous mass of floated trees of all kinds, which have lodged there. Large sand-banks have been completely removed by the impetuous whirls of the waters, and have been deposited in other places. Some appear quite new to the eye of the navigator, who has to mark their situation and bearings in his log-book.

The trees on the margins of the banks have in many parts given way. They are seen bending over the stream, like the grounded arms of an overwhelmed army of giants. Everywhere are heard the lamentations of the farmer and planter, whilst their servants and themselves are busily employed in repairing the damages occasioned by the floods. At one crevasse an old ship or two, dismantled for the purpose, are sunk, to obstruct the passage opened by the still rushing waters, while new earth is brought to fill up the chasms. The squatter is seen shouldering his rifle, and making his way through the morass, in search of his lost stock, to drive the survivors home, and save the skins of the drowned. New fences have everywhere to be formed; even new houses must be erected, to save which from a like disaster, the settler places them on an elevated platform supported by pillars made of the trunks of trees. The lands must be ploughed anew, and if the season is not too far advanced, a crop of corn and potatoes may yet be raised. But the rich prospects of the planter are blasted. The traveller is impeded in his journey, the creeks and smaller streams having broken up their banks in a degree proportionate to their size. A bank of sand, which seems firm and secure, suddenly gives way beneath the traveller's horse, and the next moment the animal has sunk in the quicksand, either to the chest in front, or over the crupper behind, leaving its master in a situation not to be envied.

Unlike the mountain-torrents and small rivers of other parts of the world, the Mississippi rises but slowly during these floods, continuing for several weeks to increase at the rate of about an inch a day. When at its height, it undergoes little fluctuation for some days, and after this subsides as slowly as it rose. The usual duration of a flood is from four to six weeks, although, on some occasions, it is protracted to two months.

Every one knows how largely the idea of floods and cataclysms enters into the speculations of the geologist. If the streamlets of the European Continent afford illustrations of the formation of strata, how much more must the Mississippi, with its ever-shifting sand-banks, its crumbling shores, its enormous masses of drift timber, the source of future beds of coal, its extensive and varied alluvial deposits, and its mighty mass of waters rolling sullenly along, like the flood of eternity!

MY VISIT TO NIAGARA

NATHANIEL HAWTHORNE

Nathaniel Hawthorne was a native of Salem, Massachusetts, a descendant of one of the Puritan families that had witnessed the Salem Witch Trials of the 1600s, which may account for his lifelong obsession with the nature of sin and redemption. His most famous novels, *The Scarlet Letter* (1850) and *The House of the Seven Gables* (1851), both set in Massachusetts, are dark and gothic. Although he was naturally reclusive, in 1832 at the age of twenty-eight he made what he called "the American Grand Tour," paying for the trip by writing magazine articles: this account of his visit to Niagara Falls was published anonymously in *New-England Magazine* in February 1835. It is a revealing account of how the mightier forces of nature challenged the nineteenth-century metaphysical mind.

. . .

AFTER DINNER—at which an unwonted and perverse epicurism detained me longer than usual—I lighted a cigar and paced the piazza, minutely attentive to the aspect and business of a very ordinary village. Finally, with reluctant step, and the feeling of an intruder, I walked towards Goat Island. At the toll-house, there were further excuses for delaying the inevitable moment. My signature was required in a huge ledger, containing similar records innumerable, many of which I read. The skin of a great sturgeon, and other fishes, beasts, and reptiles; a collection of minerals, such as lie in heaps near the falls; some Indian moccasins, and other trifles, made of deer-skin and embroidered with beads; several newspapers from Montreal, New York, and Boston; all attracted me in turn. Out of a number of twisted sticks, the manufacture of a Tuscarora Indian, I selected one of curled maple, curiously convoluted, and adorned with the carved images of a snake and a fish. Using this as my pilgrim's staff, I crossed the bridge. Above and below me were the rapids, a river of impetuous snow, with here and there a dark rock amid its whiteness, resisting all the physical fury, as any cold spirit did the moral influences of the scene. On reaching Goat Island, which separates the two great segments of the falls, I chose the right-hand path, and followed it to the edge of the American cascade. There, while the falling sheet was yet invisible, I saw the vapor that never vanishes, and the Eternal Rainbow of Niagara.

It was an afternoon of glorious sunshine, without a cloud, save those of the cataracts. I gained an insulated rock, and beheld a broad sheet of brilliant and unbroken foam, not shooting in a curved line from the top of the precipice, but falling headlong down from height to depth. A narrow stream diverged from the main branch, and hurried over the crag by a channel of its own, leaving a little pine-clad island and a streak of precipice, between itself and the larger sheet. Below arose the mist, on which was painted a dazzling sunbow, with two concentric shadows—one, almost as perfect as the original brightness; and the other, drawn faintly round the broken edge of the cloud.

Still, I had not half seen Niagara. Following the verge of the island, the path led me to the Horseshoe, where the real broad St. Lawrence, rushing along on a level with its banks, pours its whole breadth over a concave line of precipice, and thence pursues its course between lofty crags towards Ontario. A sort of bridge, two or three feet wide, stretches out along the edge of the descending sheet, and hangs upon the rising mist, as if that were the foundation of the frail structure. Here I stationed myself, in the blast of wind, which the rushing river bore along with it. The bridge was tremulous beneath me, and marked the tremor of the solid earth. I looked along the whitening rapids, and endeavored to distinguish a mass of water far above the falls, to follow it to their verge, and go down with it, in fancy, to the abyss of clouds and storm. Casting my eyes across the river, and every side, I took in the whole scene at a glance, and tried to comprehend it in one vast idea. After an hour thus spent, I left the bridge, and, by a staircase, winding almost interminably round a post, descended to the base of the precipice. From that point, my path lay over slippery stones, and among great fragments of the cliff, to the edge of the cataract, where the wind at once enveloped me in spray, and perhaps dashed the rainbow round me. Were my long desires fulfilled? And had I seen Niagara?

Oh, that I had never heard of Niagara till I beheld it. Blessed were the wanderers of old, who heard its deep roar sounding through the woods, as the summons to an unknown wonder, and approached its awful brink, in all the freshness of native feeling. Had its own mysterious voice been the first to warn me of its existence, then, indeed, I might have knelt down and worshiped. But I had come thither haunted with a vision of foam and fury, and dizzy cliffs, and an ocean tumbling down out of the sky—a scene, in short, which Nature had too much good taste and calm simplicity to realize. My mind had struggled to adapt these false conceptions to the reality, and finding the effort vain, a wretched sense of disappointment weighed me down. I climbed the precipice, and threw myself on the earth—feeling that I was unworthy to look at the Great Falls, and careless about beholding them again.

ALL THAT NIGHT, as there has been and will be, for ages past and to come, a rushing sound was heard, as if a great tempest were sweeping through the air. It mingled with my dreams, and made them full of storm and whirlwind. Whenever I awoke, and heard this dread sound in the air, and the windows rattling as with a mighty blast, I could not rest again, till, looking forth, I saw how bright the stars were, and that every leaf in the garden was motionless. Never was a summer night more calm to the eye, nor a gale of autumn louder to the ear. The rushing sound proceeds from the rapids, and the rattling of the casements is but an effect of the vibration of the whole house, shaken by the jar of the cataract. The noise of the rapids draws the attention from the true voice of Niagara, which is a dull, muffled thunder, resounding between the cliffs. I spent a wakeful hour at midnight, in distinguishing its reverberations, and rejoiced to find that my former awe and enthusiasm were reviving.

Gradually, and after much contemplation, I came to know, by my own feelings, that Niagara is indeed a wonder of the world, and not the less wonderful, because time and thought must be employed in comprehending it. Casting aside all preconceived notions, and preparation to be direstruck or delighted, the beholder must stand beside it in the simplicity of his heart, suffering the mighty scene to work its own impression. Night after night, I dreamed of it, and was gladdened every morning by the consciousness of a growing capacity to enjoy it. Yet I will not pretend to the all-absorbing enthusiasm of some more fortunate spectators, nor deny, that very trifling causes would draw my eyes and thoughts from the cataract.

The last day that I was to spend at Niagara, before my departure for the far West, I sat upon the Table Rock. This celebrated station did not now, as of old, project fifty feet beyond the line of the precipice, but was shattered by the fall of an immense fragment, which lay distant on the shore below. Still, on the utmost verge of the rock, with my feet hanging over it, I felt as if suspended in the open air. Never before had my mind been in such perfect unison with the scene. There were intervals, when I was conscious of nothing but the great river, rolling calmly into the abyss, rather descending than precipitating itself, and acquiring tenfold majesty from its unhurried motion. It came like the march of destiny. It was not taken by surprise, but seemed to have anticipated, in all its course through the broad lakes, that it must pour their collected waters down this height. The perfect foam of the river, after its descent, and the ever varying shapes of mist, rising up, to become clouds in the sky, would be the very picture of confusion, were it merely transient, like the rage of a tempest. But when the beholder has stood awhile, and perceives no lull in the storm, and considers that the vapor and the foam are as everlasting as the rocks which produce them, all this turmoil assumes a sort of calmness. It soothes, while it awes the mind.

Leaning over the cliff, I saw the guide conducting two adventurers behind the falls. It was pleasant, from that high seat in the sunshine, to observe them struggling against the eternal storm of the lower regions, with heads bent down, now faltering, now pressing forward, and finally swallowed up in their victory. After their disappearance, a blast rushed out with an old hat, which it had swept from one of their heads. The rock, to which they were directing their unseen course is marked, at a fearful distance on the exterior of the sheet, by a jet of foam. The attempt to reach it, appears both poetical and perilous, to a looker-on, but may be accomplished without much more difficulty or hazard, than in stemming a violent northeaster. In a few moments, forth came the children of the mist. Dripping and breathless, they crept along the base of the cliff, ascended to the guide's cottage, and received, I presume, a certificate of their achievement, with three verses of sublime poetry on the back.

My contemplations were often interrupted by strangers, who came down from Forsyth's to take their first view of the falls. A short, ruddy, middle-aged gentleman, fresh from old England, peeped over the rock, and evinced his approbation by a broad grin. His spouse, a very robust lady, afforded a sweet example of maternal solicitude, being so intent on the safety of her little boy that she did not even glance at Niagara. As for the child, he gave himself wholly to the enjoyment of a stick of candy. Another traveler, a native American, and no rare character among us, produced a volume of Captain Hall's tour, and labored earnestly to adjust Niagara to the captain's description, departing, at last, without one new idea or sensation of his own. The next comer was provided, not with a printed book, but with a blank sheet of foolscap, from top to bottom of which, by means of an ever-pointed pencil, the cataract was made to thunder. In a little talk, which we had together, he awarded his approbation to the general view, but censured the position of Goat Island, observing that it should have been thrown farther to the right, so as to widen the American falls, and contract those of the Horseshoe. Next appeared two traders of Michigan, who declared that, upon the whole, the sight was worth looking at; there certainly was an immense waterpower here; but that, after all, they would go twice as far to see the noble stoneworks of Lockport, where the Grand Canal is locked down a descent of sixty feet. They were succeeded by a young fellow, in homespun cotton dress, with a staff in his hand, and a pack over his shoulders. He advanced close to the edge of the rock, where his attention, at first wavering among the different components of the scene, finally became fixed in the angle of the Horseshoe falls, which is, indeed, the central point of interest. His whole soul seemed to go forth and be transported thither, till the staff slipped from his relaxed grasp, and falling down—down—struck upon the fragment of the Table Rock.

In this manner, I spent some hours, watching the varied impression made by the cataract, on those who disturbed me, and returning to unwearied contemplation, when left alone. At length, my time came to depart. There is a grassy footpath, through the woods, along the summit of the bank, to a point whence a causeway, hewn in the side of the precipice, goes winding down to the ferry, about half a mile below the Table Rock. The sun was near setting, when I emerged from the shadow of the trees, and began the descent. The indirectness of my downward road continually changed the point of view, and shewed me, in rich and repeated succession—now, the whitening rapids and the majestic leap of the main river, which appeared more deeply massive as the light departed, now, the lovelier picture, yet still sublime, of Goat Island with its rocks and grove, and the lesser falls, tumbling over the right bank of the St. Lawrence, like a tributary stream, now, the long vista of the river, as it eddied and whirled between the cliffs, to pass through Ontario towards the sea, and everywhere to be wondered at, for this one unrivalled scene. The golden sunshine tinged the sheet of the American cascade, and painted on its heaving spray the broken semicircle of a rainbow, Heaven's own beauty crowning earth's sublimity. My steps were slow, and I paused long at every turn of the descent, as one lingers and pauses, who discerns a brighter and brightening excellence in what he must soon behold no more. The solitude of the old wilderness now reigned over the whole vicinity of the falls. My enjoyment became the more rapturous, because no poet shared it—nor wretch, devoid of poetry, profaned it: But the spot, so famous through the world, was all my own!

THE LAKE OF SALT

CHARLES DARWIN

C harles Darwin was born in Shrewsbury, England, in 1809 and studied
medicine at Edinburgh University, but, as he later remarked, "the
subject disgusted me." He then went to Cambridge with the idea of becoming a clergyman; in 1831, that intention also "died a natural death when
I joined the *Beagle* as a naturalist." It was during his visit to the Galapa-
gos Islands that he pondered patterns of species distribution that formed
the basis of his concept of natural selection, later described in *The Origin
of Species* (1859). Darwin suffered from chronic seasickness and often had
Captain FitzRoy set him ashore in South America while the crew made
soundings, then pick him up weeks later farther south. It was during one of
these rambles in Argentina that he visited the salt lake described in this passage from his first book, *Journal of Researches into the Natural History and
Geology of the Countries Visited During the Voyage of H.M.S. Beagle Round
the World* (1839). His discovery of organisms living in almost pure salt con-
vinced him of the tenacity of life and the wonders of adaptation.

. . .

ONE DAY I RODE to a large salt lake, or Salina, which is distant fifteen miles from the town. During the winter it consists of a shallow lake of brine, which in summer is converted into a field of snow-white salt. The layer near the margin is from four to five inches thick, but towards the centre its thickness increases. This lake was two and a half miles long, and one broad. Others occur in the neighbourhood many times larger, and with a floor of salt, two and three feet in thickness, even when under water during the winter. One of these brilliantly white and level expanses, in the midst of the brown and desolate plain, offers an extraordinary spectacle. A large quantity of salt is annually drawn from the salina; and great piles, some hundred tons in weight, were lying ready for exportation. It is singular that the salt, although well crystallized, and appearing quite pure, does not answer so well for preserving meat as sea salt from the Cape de Verd Islands. Although the latter is necessarily much dearer, it is constantly imported and mixed with the salt procured from these salinas. A merchant at Buenos Ayres told me that he considered the Cape de Verd salt worth 50 per cent more than that from the Rio Negro. The season for working the salinas forms the harvest of Patagones; for on it, the prosperity of the place depends. Nearly the whole population encamps on the banks of the river, and the people are employed in drawing out the salt in bullock-waggons.

The border of the lake is formed of mud: and in this numerous large crystals of gypsum, some of which are three inches long, lie embedded; whilst on the surface, others of sulphate of magnesia lie scattered about. The Gauchos call the for-

mer the "Padre del sal," and the latter the "Madre"; they state
that these progenitive salts always occur on the borders of
the salinas, when the water begins to evaporate. The mud is
black, and has a fetid odour. I could not, at first, imagine the
cause of this, but I afterwards perceived that the froth, which
the wind drifted on shore, was coloured green, as if by confervae: I attempted to carry home some of this green matter, but
from an accident failed. Parts of the lake seen from a short distance appeared of a reddish colour, and this, perhaps, was owing
to some infusorial animalcula. The mud in many places was
thrown up by numbers of some kind of worm, or annelidous
animal. How surprising it is that any creatures should be able
to exist in a fluid, saturated with brine, and that they should be
crawling among crystals of sulphate of soda and lime! And what
becomes of these worms when, during a long summer, the surface at least is hardened into a solid layer of salt? Flamingoes
in considerable numbers inhabit this lake; they breed here, and
their bodies are sometimes found by the workmen, preserved
in the salt. I saw several wading about in search of food, probably for the worms which burrow in the mud; and these latter,
perhaps, feed on infusoria or confervae. Thus we have a little
world within itself, adapted to these little inland seas of brine...
Well may we affirm, that every part of the world is habitable!
Whether lakes of brine, or those subterranean ones hidden
beneath volcanic mountains—warm mineral springs; the wide
expanse and depths of the ocean; the upper regions of the atmosphere; and even the surface of perpetual snow—all support
organic beings.

THE TOCANTINS
AND CAMETÁ

HENRY WALTER BATES

The son of a Leicester hosiery manufacturer, Henry Walter Bates apprenticed in his father's business but indulged an amateur passion for insect collecting. In 1843, at the age of eighteen, he wrote a paper "On Coleopterous Insects Frequenting Damp Places" and shortly thereafter met the naturalist Alfred Russel Wallace, who shared his interest in natural history. (It would be Wallace who, in 1858, penned the paper on natural selection that spurred Darwin into hastily writing *The Origin of Species*). Bates and Wallace sailed to Brazil in 1848, intending to spend two years gathering specimens and selling them to collectors in England. They traveled up the Amazon River to its first major tributary, the Tocantins, and from there to Santarém. Wallace returned to England in 1852, but Bates stayed until 1859, returning with 14,712 species of mammals, birds, reptiles, fish, and insects, of which 8,000 were new to science. He published *The Naturalist on the River Amazons,* an early account of the dangers and excitement of natural history exploration, in 1863.

. . .

AUGUST 26TH, 1848. Mr. Wallace and I started to-day up the river Tocantins, whose mouth lies about forty-five miles in a straight line, but eighty miles following the bends of the river channels, to the south-west of Pará. This river has a course of 1,600 miles, and stands third in rank amongst the streams which form the Amazons system . . .

We set sail in the evening, after waiting several hours in vain for one of our crew. It was soon dark, the wind blew stiffly, and the tide rushed along with great rapidity, carrying us swiftly past the crowd of vessels which were anchored in the port. The canoe rolled a good deal. After we had made five or six miles of way the tide turned, and we were obliged to cast anchor. Not long after, we laid ourselves down all three together on the mat, which was spread over the floor of our cabin, and soon fell asleep.

On awaking at sunrise the next morning, we found ourselves gliding upwards with the tide, along the Bahia or Bay, as it is called, of Goajará. This is a broad channel lying between the mainland and a line of islands which extend some distance beyond the city. Into it three large rivers discharge their waters, namely, the Guamá, the Acará, and the Mojú; so that it forms a kind of sub-estuary within the grand estuary of Pará. It is nearly four miles broad. The left bank, along which we were now sailing, was beautiful in the extreme; not an inch of soil was to be seen, the water frontage presented a compact wall of rich and varied forest, resting on the surface of the stream. It seemed to form a finished border to the water scene, where the dome-like, rounded shapes of exogenous trees which constituted the mass formed the groundwork, and the endless diversity of broad-leaved Heliconiae and Palms—each kind differing in stem, crown, and fronds—the rich embroidery. The morning was calm and cloudless; and the slanting beams of the early sun, striking full on the front of the forest, lighted up the whole most gloriously. The only sound of life which reached us was the call of the Serracúra (*Gallinula cayennensis*), a kind of wild-fowl; all else was so still that the voices of boatmen could be plainly heard from canoes passing a mile or two distant from us. The sun soon gains great power on the water, but with it the sea-breeze increases in strength, moderating the heat which would otherwise be almost insupportable. We reached the end of the Goajará about midday, and then entered the narrower channel of the Mojú. Up this we travelled, partly rowing and partly sailing between the same unbroken walls of forest, until the morning of the 28th.

August 29th... On rounding a point of land, we came in full view of the Tocantins. The event was announced by one of our Indians, who was on the look-out at the prow, shouting, "La está o Paraná-uassú!" "Behold the great river!" It was a grand sight—a broad expanse of dark waters dancing merrily to the breeze; the opposite shore, a narrow blue line, miles away...

About midnight, the tide being favourable and the breeze strong, we crossed the river, taking it in a slanting direction, a distance of sixteen miles, and arrived at eight o'clock the following morning at Cametá. This is a town of some importance, pleasantly situated on the somewhat high terra firma of the left bank of the Tocantins...

The river view from Cametá is magnificent. The town is situated, as already mentioned, on a high bank, which forms quite a considerable elevation for this flat country, and the broad expanse of dark-green waters is studded with low, palm-clad islands; the prospect down river, however, being clear, or bounded only by the sea-like horizon of water and sky. The shores are washed by the breeze-tossed waters into little bays and creeks, fringed with sandy beaches. The Tocantins has been likened, by Prince Adalbert of Prussia, who crossed its mouth in 1846, to the Ganges. It is upwards of ten miles in breadth at its mouth; opposite Cametá it is five miles broad. Mr. Burchell, the well-known English traveller, descended the river from the mining provinces of interior Brazil some years before our visit. Unfortunately, the utility of this fine stream is impaired by the numerous obstructions to its navigation in the shape of cataracts and rapids, which commence, in ascending, at about 120 miles above Cametá...

September 16th. Embarked at 6 AM in a large montaria which had been lent to us for this part of our voyage by Senhor Seixas, leaving the vigilinga anchored close to a rocky islet, named Santa Anna, to await our return. At 10 AM we arrived at the first rapids, which are called Tapaiunaquára. The river, which was here about a mile wide, was choked up with rocks, a broken ridge passing completely across it. Between these confused piles of stone the currents were fearfully strong, and formed numerous eddies and whirlpools. We were obliged to get out occasionally and walk from rock to rock, whilst the men dragged the canoe over the obstacles. Beyond Tapaiunaquára, the stream became again broad and deep, and the river scenery was beautiful in the extreme. The water was clear, and of a bluish-green colour. On both sides of the stream stretched ranges of wooded hills, and in the middle picturesque islets rested on the smooth water, whose brilliant green woods fringed with palms formed charming bits of foreground to the perspective of sombre hills fading into grey in the distance. Joaquim pointed out to us grove after grove of Brazil-nut trees (*Bertholletia excelsa*) on the mainland. This is one of the chief collecting grounds for this nut. The tree is one of the loftiest in the forest, towering far above its fellows; we could see the woody fruits, large and round as cannon-balls, dotted over the branches. The currents were very strong in some places, so that during the greater part of the way the men preferred to travel near the shore, and propel the boat by means of long poles.

We arrived at Arroyos about four o'clock in the afternoon, after ten hours' hard pull...We dined ashore, and in the evening again embarked to visit the falls. The vigorous and successful way in which our men battled with the terrific currents excited our astonishment. The bed of the river, here about a mile wide, is strewn with blocks of various sizes, which lie in the most irregular manner, and between them rush currents of more or less rapidity. With an accurate knowledge of the place and skilful management, the falls can be approached in small canoes by threading the less dangerous channels. The main fall is about a quarter of a mile wide; we climbed to an elevation overlooking it, and had a good view of the cataract. A body of water rushes

with terrific force down a steep slope, and boils up with deaf-
ening roar round the boulders which obstruct its course. The
wildness of the whole scene was very impressive. As far as the
eye could reach, stretched range after range of wooded hills and
scores of miles of beautiful wilderness, inhabited only by scanty
tribes of wild Indians. In the midst of such a solitude, the roar of
the cataract seemed fitting music...

September 26th. At length we got clear of the islands, and
saw once more before us the sea-like expanse of waters which
forms the mouth of the Tocantins. The river had now sunk to its
lowest point, and numbers of fresh-water dolphins were rolling
about in shoaly places. There are here two species, one of which
was new to science when I sent specimens to England; it is called
the Tucuxí (*Steno tucuxi* of Gray). When it comes to the surface
to breathe, it rises horizontally, showing first its back fin; draws
an inspiration, and then dives gently down, head foremost. This
mode of proceeding distinguishes the Tucuxí at once from the
other species, which is called Bouto or porpoise by the natives
(*Inia geoffroyi* of Desmarest). When this rises the top of the head
is the part first seen; it then blows, and immediately afterwards
dips head downwards, its back curving over, exposing succes-
sively the whole dorsal ridge with its fin. It seems thus to pitch
heels over head, but does not show the tail fin. Besides this pecu-
liar motion, it is distinguished from the Tucuxí by its habit of
generally going in pairs. Both species are exceedingly numerous
throughout the Amazons and its larger tributaries, but they are
nowhere more plentiful than in the shoaly water at the mouth

of the Tocantins, especially in the dry season. In the Upper Amazons a third pale flesh-coloured species is also abundant (the *Delphinus pallidus* of Gervais). With the exception of a species found in the Ganges, all other varieties of dolphin inhabit exclusively the sea. In the broader parts of the Amazons, from its mouth to a distance of fifteen hundred miles in the interior, one or other of the three kinds here mentioned are always heard rolling, blowing, and snorting, especially at night, and these noises contribute much to the impression of sea-wide vastness and desolation which haunts the traveller. Besides dolphins in the water, frigate birds in the air are characteristic of this lower part of the Tocantins. Flocks of them were seen the last two or three days of our journey, hovering above at an immense height. Towards night, we were obliged to cast anchor over a shoal in the middle of the river to await the ebb tide. The wind blew very strongly, and this, together with the incoming flow, caused such a heavy sea that it was impossible to sleep. The vessel rolled and pitched until every bone in our bodies ached with the bumps we received, and we were all more or less sea-sick. On the following day we entered the Anapú, and on the 30th of September, after threading again the labyrinth of channels communicating between the Tocantins and the Moju, arrived at Pará.

GANGES,
THE GREAT PURIFIER

MARK TWAIN

S amuel Langhorne Clemens ("Mark Twain" was a pseudonym, from a
call given by riverboatsmen when sounding the shallows of the Mississippi River) was born in Florida, Missouri, in 1835. In his late twenties
he went to Nevada to become secretary to his brother, who worked for the
governor of that state, and later to Buffalo, New York, where he became a
newspaper editor. He moved to Hartford, Connecticut, and wrote the two
novels that have become quintessential American classics: *The Adventures of
Tom Sawyer* (1876) and *The Adventures of Huckleberry Finn* (1884). Always a
great traveler and a popular speaker, he had a sharp eye for pretentiousness
and an even sharper tongue for exposing it. He was, however, a poor busi-
nessman and in 1893 went into bankruptcy after investing in a typesetting
machine that didn't work. To earn money, he set out on a lecture tour that
took him around the world; this description of India's Ganges River, with
its fascinating blend of the sacred and the profane, is from his account of the
tour, *Following the Equator*, published in 1897.

. . .

THE GANGES FRONT is the supreme show-place of Benares. Its tall bluffs are solidly caked from water to summit, along a stretch of three miles, with a splendid jumble of massive and picturesque masonry, a bewildering and beautiful confusion of stone platforms, temples, stair-flights, rich and stately palaces— nowhere a break, nowhere a glimpse of the bluff itself; all the long face of it is compactly walled from sight by this crammed perspective of platforms, soaring stairways, sculptured temples, majestic palaces, softening away into the distances; and there is movement, motion, human life everywhere, and brilliantly costumed—streaming in rainbows up and down the lofty stairways, and massed in metaphorical flower-gardens on the miles of great platforms at the river's edge...

We made the usual trip up and down the river, seated in chairs under an awning on the deck of the usual commodious hand-propelled ark; made it two or three times, and could have made it with increasing interest and enjoyment many times more; for, of course, the palaces and temples would grow more and more beautiful every time one saw them, for that happens with all such things; also, I think one would not get tired of the bathers, nor their costumes, nor of their ingenuities in getting out of them and into them again without exposing too much bronze, nor of their devotional gesticulations and absorbed bead-tellings.

But I should get tired of seeing them wash their mouths with that dreadful water and drink it. In fact, I did get tired of it, and very early, too. At one place where we halted for a while, the foul gush from a sewer was making the water turbid and murky all around, and there was a random corpse slopping around in it that had floated down from up country. Ten steps below that place stood a crowd of men, women, and comely young maidens waist-deep in the water—and they were scooping it up in their hands and drinking it. Faith can certainly do wonders, and this is an instance of it. Those people were not drinking that fearful stuff to assuage thirst, but in order to purify their souls and the interior of their bodies. According to their creed, the Ganges water makes everything pure that it touches—instantly and utterly pure. The sewer-water was not an offense to them, the corpse did not revolt them; the sacred water had touched both, and both were now snow-pure, and could defile no one. The memory of that sight will always stay by me; but not by request.

A word further concerning the nasty but all-purifying Ganges water. When we went to Agra, by and by, we happened there just in time to be in at the birth of a marvel—a memorable scientific discovery—the discovery that in certain ways the foul and derided Ganges water *is* the most puissant purifier in the world! This curious fact, as I have said, had just been added to the treasury of modern science. It had long been noted as a strange thing that while Benares is often afflicted with the cholera she does not spread it beyond her borders. This could not be accounted for. Mr. Henkin, the scientist in the employ of the government of Agra, concluded to examine the water. He went to Benares and made his tests. He got water at the mouths of the sewers where they empty into the river at the bathing-ghats; a cubic centimeter of it contained millions of germs; at the end of six hours they were *all dead*. He caught a floating corpse, towed it to the shore, and from beside it he dipped up water that was swarming with cholera germs; at the end of six hours they were *all dead*. He added swarm after swarm of cholera germs to this water; within the six hours *they always died*, to the last sample. Repeatedly, he took pure well-water which was barren of animal life, and put into it a few cholera germs; they always began to propagate at once, and always within six hours they swarmed— and were numerable by *millions upon millions*.

For ages and ages the Hindus have had absolute faith that the water of the Ganges was absolutely pure, could not be defiled by any contact whatsoever, and infallibly made pure and clean whatsoever thing touched it. They still believe it, and that is why they bathe in it and drink it, caring nothing for its *seeming* filthiness and the floating corpses. The Hindus have been laughed at, these many generations, but the laughter will need to modify itself a little from now on. How did they find out the water's secret in those ancient ages? Had they germ-scientists then? We do not know. We only know that they had a civilization long before we emerged from savagery.

THE SOURCE OF
THE ALBERTINE NILE

HENRY MORTON STANLEY

Born John Rowlands in Denbigh, Wales, Stanley sailed as a cabin boy to New Orleans in 1859; there he was adopted by a merchant named Stanley. In 1867, he became a reporter for the *New York Herald*, and two years later was ordered by the paper's publisher to go to Africa to find the Scottish explorer David Livingstone. Livingstone, who was not lost, was making a third unsuccessful attempt to discover the source of the Nile— Stanley "found" him on the Congo River in November, 1871. In 1879, Stanley returned to Africa to help found the Congo Free State, and it was during this campaign that he stumbled upon the mist-shrouded Lake Albert Edward, described in this excerpt from *In Darkest Africa* (1890). The lake turned out to be the long-sought source of the Blue, or Albertine, Nile.

. . .

OUR FIRST VIEW, as well as the last, of Lake Albert Edward, was utterly unlike any view we ever had before of land or water of a new region. For all other virgin scenes were seen through a more or less clear atmosphere, and we saw the various effects of sunshine, and were delighted with the charms which distance lends. On this, however, we gazed through fluffy, slightly waving strata of vapours of unknown depth, and through this thick opaque veil the lake appeared like dusty quicksilver, or a sheet of lustreless silver, bounded by vague shadowy outlines of a tawny-faced land. It was most unsatisfying in every way. We could neither define distance, form, or figure, estimate height of land-crests above the water, or depth of lake; we could ascribe no just limit to the extent of the expanse, nor venture to say whether it was an inland ocean or a shallow pond. The haze, or rather cloud, hung over it like a grey pall. We sighed for rain to clear the atmosphere, and the rain fell; but, instead of thickened haze, there came a fog as dark as that which distracts London on a November day.

The natural colour of the lake is of a light sea-green colour, but at a short distance from the shore it is converted by the unfriendly mist into that of pallid grey, or sackcloth. There is neither sunshine nor sparkle, but a dead opacity, struggling through a measureless depth of mist. If we attempted to peer under or through it, to get a peep at the mysterious water, we were struck with the suggestion of chaos at the sight of the pallid surface, brooding under the trembling and seething atmosphere. It realized perfectly the description that "in the beginning the earth was without form and void, and darkness was upon the face of the deep."

This idea was strengthened when we looked up to examine the composition of this vaporous mist, and to ascertain whether we might call it haze, mist, or fog. The eyes were fascinated with the clouds of fantastic and formless phantasms, the eerie figures, flakes, films, globules, and frayed or wormlike threads, swimming and floating and drifting in such numberless multitudes that one fancied he could catch a handful. In the delirium of fevers I have often seen such shapes, like wriggling animalculae, shifting their forms with the rapidity of thought, and swiftly evolving into strange amorphous figures before the dazed senses. More generally, and speaking plainly, the atmosphere seemed crowded with shadowy, elongated organisms, the most frequent bearing a rough resemblance to squirming tadpoles. While looking at the dim image of an island about three miles from the shore, it was observed that the image deepened, or got more befogged, as a thinner or thicker horizontal stratum of these atmospheric shapes subsided downward or floated upward; and following this with a fixed sight, I could see a vibration of it as clearly as of a stream of sunbeams. From the crest of a grassy ridge and the crown of a tall hill, and the sad grey beach, I tried to resolve what was imaged but three miles away, and to ascertain whether it was tawny land, or grey water, or ashen sky, but all in vain. I needed but to hear the distant strains of a dirge to cause me to imagine that one of Kakuri's canoes out yonder on the windless lake was a funereal barge, slowly gliding with its freight of dead explorers to the gloomy bourne from whence never an explorer returned.

And oh! what might have been seen had we but known one of those marvellously clear days, with the deep purified azure and that dazzling transparency of ether so common to New York! We might have set some pictures before the world from these never-known lands as never painter painted. We might have been able to show the lake, with its tender blue colour, here broadening nobly, there enfolding with its sparkling white arms clusters of tropic isles, or projecting long silvery tongues of blazing water into the spacious meadowy flats, curving everywhere in rounded bays, or extending along flowing shore-lines, under the shadows of impending plateau walls, and flotillas of canoes gliding over its bright bosom to give it life, and broad green bands of marsh grasses, palms, plantains, waving crops of sugar-cane, and umbrageous globes of foliage, to give beauty to its borders. And from point to point round about the compass we could have shown the irregularly circular line of lofty uplands, their proud hill bosses rising high into the clear air, and their mountainous promontories, with their domed crowns projected far into the basin, or receding into deep folds half enclosing fair valleys, and the silver threads of streams shooting in arrowy flights down the cliffy steeps; broad bands of vivid green grass, and spaces of deep green forest, alternating with frowning grey or white precipices, and far northward the horizon bounded by the Alps of Ruwenzori, a league in height above the lake, beautiful in their pure white garments of snow, entrancingly picturesque in their congregation of peaks and battalions of mountain satellites ranged gloriously against the crystalline sky.

But alas! alas! In vain we turned our yearning eyes and longing looks in their direction. The Mountains of the Moon lay ever slumbering in their cloudy tents, and the lake which gave birth to the Albertine Nile remained ever brooding under the impenetrable and loveless mist.

SPECKLED TROUT

JOHN BURROUGHS

John Burroughs was born near Roxbury, New York, in 1837, the seventh of ten siblings. At the age of seven he saw an unfamiliar bird—it turned out to be a black-throated blue warbler—and remained fascinated by nature for the rest of his life. He became a teacher at a school near West Point, New York, where he met Ralph Waldo Emerson, who encouraged him to write, and where he saw the works of Audubon, which further fired his love of natural history. In 1861 he began publishing essays in the *New York Leader*, and in 1863 he moved to Washington, D.C., where he worked for the Treasury Department while still writing on wildlife subjects. The depiction of nature in his first book, *Wake-Robin* (1871) was clearly influenced by Darwin. His subsequent nature articles in *The Atlantic* drew the admiration of millions. He was a passionate, gentle observer of the natural environment, as is shown in this excerpt from the essay "Speckled Trout," written in 1903. He died in Ohio, on his way home to the Catskills, after visiting Alaska with John Muir in March 1921.

• • •

I HAVE BEEN A SEEKER of trout from my boyhood, and on all the expeditions in which this fish has been the ostensible purpose I have brought home more game than my creel showed. In fact, in my mature years I find I got more of nature into me, more of the woods, the wild, nearer to bird and beast, while threading my native streams for trout, than in almost any other way. It furnished a good excuse to go forth; it pitched one in the right key; it sent one through the fat and marrowy places of field and wood. Then the fisherman has a harmless, preoccupied look; he is a kind of vagrant that nothing fears. He blends himself with the trees and the shadows. All his approaches are gentle and indirect. He times himself to the meandering, soliloquizing stream; its impulse bears him along. At the foot of the waterfall he sits sequestered and hidden in its volume of sound. The birds know he has no designs upon them, and the animals see that his mind is in the creek. His enthusiasm anneals him and makes him pliable to the scenes and influences he moves among.

Then what acquaintance he makes with the stream! He addresses himself to it as a lover to his mistress; he wooes it and stays with it till he knows its most hidden secrets. It runs through his thoughts not less than through its banks there; he feels the fret and thrust of every bar and boulder. Where it deepens, his purpose deepens; where it is shallow, he is indifferent. He knows how to interpret its every glance and dimple; its beauty haunts him for days.

I am sure I run no risk of overpraising the charm and attractiveness of a well-fed trout stream, every drop of water in it as bright and pure as if the nymphs had brought it all the way from its source in crystal goblets, and as cool as if it had been hatched beneath a glacier. When the heated and soiled and jaded refugee from the city first sees one, he feels as if he would like to turn it into his bosom and let it flow through him a few hours, it suggests such healing freshness and newness. How his roily thoughts would run clear; how the sediment would go downstream! Could he ever have an impure or an unwholesome wish afterward? The next best thing he can do is to tramp along its banks and surrender himself to its influence. If he reads it intently enough, he will, in a measure, be taking it into his mind and heart, and experiencing its salutary ministrations.

LAKE ONTARIO

RUPERT BROOKE

Rupert Chawner Brooke was born in Rugby, England (where his father was a schoolmaster), and his first book of poems was published while he was a student at Cambridge in 1911. In 1912–13 he traveled to the U.S., Canada, and Tahiti and wrote letters about his journey that were published in the *Westminster Gazette* and later collected in the book *Letters from America* (1916), from which the following description of Lake Ontario is taken. During the First World War he fought in the Netherlands; in 1915 he was killed on his way to the Dardanelles, and he was buried on Skyros, Greece. His collection of war sonnets, published a year earlier, established him as one of the best of the British war poets. Like his poems, his travel essays are lively, irreverent, and full of the sardonic, modern self-confidence that Henry James, in his preface to *Letters from America,* found "at once radiant and reflective." Brooke's pieces, he wrote, were drawn "from the very wealth of our own conscience and the very force of our own history."

. . .

THE WISE TRAVELLER from Ottawa to Toronto catches a boat at Prescott, and puffs judicially between two nations up the St. Lawrence and across Lake Ontario. We were a cosmopolitan, middle-class bunch (it is the one distinction between the Canadian and American languages that Canadians tend to say "bunch" but Americans "crowd"), out to enjoy the scenery. For this stretch of the river is notoriously picturesque, containing the Thousand Isles. The Thousand Isles vary from six inches to hundreds of yards in diameter. Each, if big enough, has been bought by a rich man—generally an American—who has built a castle on it. So the whole isn't much more beautiful than Golder's Green. We picked our way carefully between the islands. The Americans on board sat in rows saying "That house was built by Mr. ———. Made his money in biscuits. Cost three hundred thousand dollars, e-recting that building. Yessir." The Canadians sat looking out the other way, and said, "In nineteen-ten this land was worth twenty thousand an acre; now it's worth forty-five thousand. Next year. . ." and their eyes grew solemn as the eyes of men who think deep and holy thoughts. But the English sat quite still, looking straight in front of them, thinking of nothing at all, and hoping that nobody would speak to them. So we fared; until, well on in the afternoon, we came to the entrance of Lake Ontario.

There is something ominous and unnatural about these great lakes. The sweet flow of a river, and the unfriendly restless vitality of the sea, men may know and love. And the little lakes we have in Europe are but as fresh-water streams that have married and settled down, alive and healthy and comprehensible. Rivers (except the Saguenay) are human. The sea, very properly, will not be allowed in heaven. It has no soul. It is unvintageable, cruel, treacherous, what you will. But, in the end—while we have it with us—it is all right; even though that all-rightness result but, as with France, from the recognition of an age-long feud and an irremediable lack of sympathy. But these monstrous lakes, which ape the ocean, are not proper to fresh water or salt. They have souls, perceptibly, and wicked ones.

We steamed out, that day, over a flat, stationary mass of water, smooth with the smoothness of metal or polished stone or one's finger-nail. There was a slight haze everywhere. The lake was a terrible dead-silver colour, the gleam of its surface shot with flecks of blue and a vapoury enamel-green. It was like a gigantic silver shield. Its glint was inexplicably sinister and dead, like the glint on glasses worn by a blind man. In front the steely mist hid the horizon, so that the occasional rock or little island and the one ship in sight seemed hung in air. They were reflected to a preternatural length in the glassy floor. Our boat appeared to leave no wake; those strange waters closed up foamlessly behind her. But our black smoke hung, away back on the trail, in a thick, clearly-bounded cloud, becalmed in the hot, windless air, very close over the water, like an evil soul after death that cannot win dissolution. Behind us and to the right lay the low, woody shores of Southern Ontario and Prince Edward Peninsula, long dark lines of green, stretching thinner and thinner, interminably, into the distance. The lake around us was dull, though the sun shone full on it. It gleamed, but without radiance.

THE THAMES

The son of German-speaking parents who settled in Terre Haute, Indiana, Theodore Dreiser worked at the *Chicago Globe* before moving to New York in 1894 with the intention of writing novels. *Sister Carrie* appeared in 1900, but its gritty realism at a time of what he called "English sentimentalism" prevented it from becoming popular. His best-known novel, *An American Tragedy* (1925), used an actual murder case from 1906 to underscore the inevitable perversion of the American Dream that was the theme of most of his writing. In 1912, Dreiser traveled to England, France, and Italy. "I felt curiously at this time as though I was on the edge of a great change." His book about the trip, *A Traveler at Forty,* from which this description of the Thames River and its denizens is taken, appeared in 1913 and was the first of a series of autobiographical nonfiction books, including *A Hoosier Holiday* (1916), *A Book About Myself* (1922), and *Dawn* (1931). He is credited with having introduced a tough, unadorned, cynical style of writing that now almost defines American realism.

. . .

AS PLEASING HOURS as any that I spent in London were connected with the Thames—a murky little stream above London Bridge, compared with such vast bodies as the Hudson and the Mississippi, but utterly delightful. I saw it on several occasions—once in a driving rain off London Bridge, where twenty thousand vehicles were passing in the hour, it was said; once afterward at night when the boats below were faint, wind-driven lights and the crowd on the bridge black shadows. I followed it in the rain from Blackfriars Bridge, to the giant plant of the General Electric Company at Chelsea one afternoon, and thought of Sir Thomas More, and Henry VIII, who married Anne Boleyn at the Old Church near Battersea Bridge, and wondered what they would think of this modern powerhouse. What a change from Henry VIII and Sir Thomas More to vast, whirling electric dynamos and a London subway system!

Another afternoon, bleak and rainy, I reconnoitered the section lying between Blackfriars Bridge and Tower Bridge and found it very interesting from a human, to say nothing of a river, point of view; I question whether in some ways it is not the most interesting region in London, though it gives only occasional glimpses of the river...

It was interesting to me to think that I was in the center of so much that was old, but for the exact details I confess I cared little. Here the Thames was especially delightful. It presented such odd vistas. I watched the tumbling tide of water, whipped by gusty wind where moderate-sized tugs and tows were going by in the mist and rain. It was delicious, artistic, far more significant than quiescence and sunlight could have made it. I took note of the houses, the doorways, the quaint, winding passages, but for the color and charm they did not compare with the nebulous, indescribable mass of working boys and girls and men and women which moved before my gaze. The mouths of many of them were weak, their noses snub, their eyes squint, their chins undershot, their ears stub, their chests flat. Most of them had a waxy, meaty look, but for interest they were incomparable. American working crowds may be much more chipper, but not more interesting. I could not weary of looking at them.

Lastly I followed the river once more all the way from Cleopatra's Needle to Chelsea one heavily downpouring afternoon and found its mood varying splendidly though never once was it anything more than black-gray, changing at times from a pale or almost sunlit yellow to a solid leaden-black hue. It looked at times as though something remarkable were about to happen, so weirdly greenish-yellow was the sky above the water; and the tall chimneys of Lambeth over the way, appearing and disappearing in the mist, were irresistible. There is a certain kind of barge which plies up and down the Thames with a collapsible mast and sail which looks for all the world like something off the Nile. These boats harmonize with the smoke and the gray, lowery skies. I was never weary of looking at them in the changing light and mist and rain. Gulls skimmed over the water here very freely all the way from Blackfriars to Battersea, and along the Embankment they sat in scores, solemnly cogitating the state of the weather, perhaps. I was delighted with the picture they made in places, greedy, wide-winged, artistic things.

THE ST. LAWRENCE

HENRY BESTON

Massachusetts born and Harvard educated, Henry Beston taught for a year in Lyon, France, before returning to Harvard in 1914 as an assistant professor of English. He joined the French Army in 1915 and, like Ernest Hemingway, served in the ambulance service, an experience related in his first book, *A Volunteer Poilu*. After the war he wrote two books of fairy tales. He remained "somewhat of a wanderer," but in 1925 he had a small cottage, "the Fo'castle," built on Cape Cod and lived in it for a year, during which he wrote his most famous nonfiction work, *The Outermost House* (1928). The next year he married Elizabeth Coatsworth, and they moved to a farm near Nobleboro, Maine, where the couple lived until Beston's death in 1968. In 1942 he wrote *The St. Lawrence*, a vivid account of the history and beauty of the river that drains the Great Lakes, for Farrar and Rinehart's Rivers of America series. Beston was named the third winner of the Emerson-Thoreau Medal by the American Academy of Arts and Sciences; the first two had gone to T.S. Eliot and Robert Frost.

. . .

UNDER A VAST LAND SKY, milky-pale with a universal tissue of cloud, the great fresh-water sea rolls before the west wind towards the narrowing and approaching shores which begin the river. The pale waves of Ontario diminish as the wind crowds them into the St. Lawrence, and a thunderstorm of early afternoon touches the dark American green of the nearer woods with silver and a veil of rain. Save for the gulls who follow beside the ship, there seem few birds.

In its great departure, the river is itself something of another lake, flowing in vague and enormous motion to the east. Indeed the whole rhythm of the landscape has an eastward resolution, with its tree shapes and its tree boughs streaming backward, and the river itself moving eastward below both current and wave. Shores of fields and hardwoods in their midsummer greenery presently gather a blacker and old-fashioned wildness, and the stream surprisingly becomes a whole inland sea of fanciful isles and archipelagoes. The Thousand Islands (the phrase has touched the American imagination) are here for the counting. Some are mere rocks emerging from the stream, poising one resolute small tree in a crevice of grey stone, some are rural felicities of field and tree with the river as a moat, others are solitaries set apart, each like a lonely star. The houses which crown them are the comfortable houses of a comfortable past, but here and there one ventures into a realm of turreted and shingled castles which is fairy land as the American fancy of the seventies and eighties saw it with perhaps a little help from Tennyson. Currents stir in the seeming lake, flowing visibly between the isles:

the river is gaining strength. At the water's edge, on polished shelves of stone, gatherings of the common tern stand massed in feathered whiteness, sheltering from the wind.

These waters might cover the entire earth so much do they seem without definition or bound. A narrow passage ultimately leads from them into the next great phase of the stream.

It is the York State St. Lawrence, the river with Ontario and Britain to one side, and the United States and Congress and the presidents to the other. To the Canadian north are old farms and fields with willows bordering their shores and silvering in the wind. Here and there, in crannies of the bank under a decorum of leaves, are old-fashioned cottages playful with architectural gingerbread, and from time to time appear small rustic towns whose houses and trees seem to have been planted together in some Canadian moment of the mid-Victorian mood. The landscape reflects a way of life less hurried than the American. Town halls have even something of a British propriety, and the bells in the brick churches strike noon with a measured and English air.

Across the stream, under the same inland light, the same level distances of grassland and trees fall back from the yellow earth of the New York shore. The farms seem more scattered and uneven and are farther from the river, towns count for less, and there are more groves of elms standing green beside the bank. It is not the landscape of the shores, however, which now seizes upon the imagination of the traveler. For thirty miles he has been following a great and single channel direct as some vast canal, a line of water drawn across a part of North America as it might be across the face of Mars. So evenly between its banks does it keep its average width of a fair two miles that the long, natural perspective has even something of an artificial air; one might be in the presence of some great work of the ancient and mysterious America of the Mound Builders. Looking westward from Prescott in Ontario one sees a surprising sight at the far end of the fairway. It is a sealike horizon on a river, a level line of water and sky suspended in space between the substantiality of parallel shores, themselves vanishing over the rounding plunge of earth.

Flat wavelets speckle the channel, flicked from the current by the inland breeze. Eastward and ahead, vast steps in the rush of the river downhill from the lakes, lie the great rapids, the roar of their narrow caldrons, long slopes, and wider seas of fury soon to break upon the listening ear.

Only the strong current, eddying in deep mid-channel and flowing like a long and hastening ripple past the banks, carries a hint of what is presently to come. The river has quickened pace into new country, an open tableland of grass and gravel down whose yellow banks glacial boulders have here and there rolled to the water's edge; the great main channel is over and done; ahead, level islands of the stream's own making bar and turn it in its gathering and meandering rush. It is farming land, and there are cattle on the islands, black-and-white Holsteins feeding under the willows and the grovelike beauty of the elms. A touch or two of industrialism on the Canadian side, and the beginning there of the canal world does not change the character of the landscape or the emphasis of its way of life. The river, which at Prescott and Ogdensburg was a pale and inland blue, has in this yellower earth gathered a tinge of green.

Lake freighters coming and going to Montreal have gone into the canals. Slow dignities of hulk and painted iron, they move along the separate water, their stacks visible in the distance above and through the trees.

The islands are now close at hand, lying in the stream like hindrances in a corridor, and confusing the descent with turns and passages about and between their steeper-growing banks. Alongside, the water is now plunging forward in a rush, boiling up from below in circles like huge lily pads expanding. Two rapids which are little more than a new and fiercer hurrying under the keel pass by without drama of sight or sound. More rapids follow and a long rush at whose far end a growing roar overflows into the blue and casual day.

A shudder, a strange motion downhill into a vast confusion and a vaster sound, and one is in the pool which is the climax of the rapids of the Long Sault. So steep is the winding rush downslope into the pool and out of it along a furious curve that the rims of water close along the banks stand higher than the tumult in the pit, and one passes, as it were, through banks of water as well as banks of land. Currents and agitations of wind, rapids of the invisible air, enclose the ship in a leap, scurrying the deck with their small and wild unrest. In the caldrons all is giant and eternal din, a confusion and war and leaping-up of white water in every figure and fury of its elemental being, the violence roaring in a ceaseless and universal hue and cry of water in all its sounds and tongues. The forms of water rising and falling here, onrushing, bursting, and dissolving, have little kinship with waves at sea, with those long bodies of the ocean's pulse. They are shapes of violence and the instancy of creation, towering pyramids crested with a splash of white, rising only to topple upstream as the downcurrent rushes at their base. Lifted for an instant of being into a beauty of pure form and the rising curve, they resemble nothing so much as the decorative and symbolic waves of the artists of Japan.

Enclosing the pool, in a strange contrast of mood, stands an almost sylvan scene, a country shore of grass and trees and a noontide restfulness of shade.

A bold turn of a gravel promontory, and one escapes out of the caldron into a broading reach of calmer water. Widening, widening to a lake, the river achieves an afternoon peace, and there comes slowly into view a landscape so much part of the old beauty of the past, a landscape so poignantly and profoundly American, that time seems to have stood still awhile above the river.

FALLING WATER

DONALD CULROSS PEATTIE

A native of Chicago and a Harvard-trained biologist, Donald Culross
Peattie worked briefly as a botanist with the U.S. Department of
Agriculture. In 1923 he married the novelist Louise Redfield, and after liv-
ing in France they settled in Louise's family's home, Redfield House, on
a large homestead nine miles from Chicago. While there, Peattie wrote a
book about nature, *An Almanac for Moderns* (1935), Louise wrote the novel
American Acres (1936), and they collaborated on a book about Redfield, *The
Happy Kingdom* (1935). Shortly thereafter, they moved to California, where
Peattie published *A Natural History of Trees of Eastern and Central North
America* (1950) and *A Natural History of Western Trees* (1953). Peattie's
trance-like description of a small waterfall and a lone dipper is excerpted
from *The Road of a Naturalist* (1941), a book partly intended as an argu-
ment for maintaining a connection with nature in a nation preparing to take
part in the Second World War.

. . .

THE WEST IS ABRUPT. Its geology and climate have sharp margins. So that, suddenly as pushing through a gate, we found ourselves in late afternoon escaped from barrens like those outside of Eden. Slant rays laddered the lofty shade. That arid gale darkened with dust had become no more than a fresh breath ploughing steady as the trades through boughs down-sweeping from the spires of giant evergreens. It carried odours of well-watered fern, of cedar sap, of needles smelling like tangerine peel, and a reviving thought of the sea. Born of the sea, washed through a million resinous leaves, this wind was dustless, colourless, pure as belief in an invisible God after an age spent with dancing demons. Dusty ourselves and blown to confusion, we felt forgiven as we skimmed along through the long light and the shadows. We felt rewarded, beyond reason, when we were shown to our room in a fine old hostel (one of the few on our journey; we use, like everybody else, the West's excellent motor cabins).

The room was a corner one, on the top floor; it was pleasing as a chamber in one's own home. But more than airy curtains and white beds made it fresh. There was a presence here that I have known caught in an old stone spring-house, or on the undersides of willow leaves. It was both a light and a sound. Across the ceiling fled constantly the ripple marks of sunshine on a current, and when I flung the window up the breeze washed in the singing of a waterfall. There just below me it plunged, arched over by leaves. The room, like the inside of a violin belly, resounded with its voice. Tired, I lay a long time listening, under the billow of the light curtain, watching the ripple marks follow each other like the years of a happy man's life.

Now when I find a waterfall right outside my door, a fall with a rainbow in it, I will tell any man I have come home, and if he wants to see me he can follow me there to find me. If he has something better to say than the cascade, let him say it; otherwise he may hold his peace.

So next morning I went to meet my falls. I forget time, both the fullness of an hour and the briefness of life, when I walk into this spell. For the pulsing flight of a cascade is hypnotic; it for ever passes and never changes. Not alive, it is nevertheless a picture of life. Every flung drop in it is individual, come flowing out of remote springs in the mass of the mountains, and drawn inevitably into this eddy. For one moment the onrushing stream is caught and wrought into a shape; the next instant that water which shattered the light in a prismatic arc has vanished into oblivion, down and away to the ultimate inertia of the sea bottom. More water for ever enters and leaves; the form of the eddy alone remains, veering a little on the wind this way and that like a dancer, but always righting to the norm. Yet it has no existence apart from the drops that compose it.

And like a living body, this waterfall is a sudden outburst of energy. Not primal astronomical power which is terrible and eternal, but an earthly revival of it on a scale human as things go in the universe, a definitely shaped impounding of a great current strength, a kinetic expression of it, with a niche in space of its own. And you can, if you wish to harness it, turn the spilled energy into light and warmth and driving purpose, as you may burn a great tree, or set a man to thinking. Or you may leave it free to dance, and still its power is not wasted, any more than it is wasting solar radiation to lock it up in the shape of a fern which no one ever discovers. In being itself, the bracken is its own end and reason.

So, content, I watched the lovely water fall and fall, leaning just over the plunge with my elbows on a sheer stone wall. My wife came out, perhaps to tell me that we should make haste for something, but she forgot what, folding her arms on the wall beside me, watching the water, finding out how there was, after all, plenty of time. We all have time for what we want in this life. Or we should have, God knows, for we shall not want it long. A young man can make the time for a girl; a good woman always has time for a child. And a naturalist will take time for a bird, as long as the bird will stay to be watched or let itself be followed. It is not surprising that one of the last naturalists to see a passenger pigeon pursued it through the woods of North Carolina a whole day. Or that there is at present one man who spends his entire time watching what may be the last thirty-four California condors left in the world. True that he has a subvention for so doing, with the high motivating purpose that study may yet save the largest and most unlikely bird in all America. But penniless ornithologists have done as much, without money or appointment for it, and for birds less rare. That is how we all know what we do about Nature or anything in science. Newton resolved a problem in physics, so he said, "by thinking of it all the time."

Now into the narrow field of my concentration flew the bird which is the very fellow of such falls as this. The water ouzel, called the dipper, is never seen apart from just such foaming rapids and singing cataracts. As the sanderling is the bird of the shoreline, skittering for ever back and forth in the drifting castles of foam, as the storm-petrel is the embodiment of mid-ocean loneliness, having no spot to rest save on the seething hills of brine, so the quick dipper belongs to the rush of fresh waters. Even a petrel must come to land to nest; it cannot, like the fabulous halcyon, rear its brood upon the sea in the unnatural calm that follows the equinox. Dippers fit with the most exquisite precision into their habitat; they live and die within a mile or less of the spot where they were hatched. Their world is a linear one, only a few feet wider than the mountain stream that they inhabit. Even in winter they migrate only so far as the nearest hole in the ice.

And perfect as a dipper seems to find his life, he is oddly made for it. Though he has not the long legs of a wader, he spends his time a-wading. Though he has no webs between his toes, he can swim; chunky, he yet can dive like the stream-lined grebe, and without long wings, still fly under water like the loon. Short of wing and stumpy of tail, round of middle as a wren, with short legs and long slender toes made as if for perch-ing, the dipper is a land bird by every anatomical feature. But by an incredible plasticity, by sheer defiance of function over struc-ture, by an adaptation that looks like will, he is an aquatic bird. He loves what I love—"white water," forest depths. He loves a stream so pure that a man can drink of it thoughtlessly, a child can see each grain of hornblende and pyrite on its bed. A river in its freshest youth, where caddis worms and stone-flies and dobsons live. And over the singing of all such western waters rises the dipper's voice, in wild contentment.

But the voice I heard above the fall this morning was a frantic baby peeping—the call of a hungering youngster who sees his mother's approach. At the roots of a fir which the water laved just before it toppled into the cascade, teetered a top-heavy fledgling dipper, craning hopefully over the perilous foam. And at the moment I perceived him, a light shadow, a swirl of slate-grey wings returned, the parent with a long aquatic larva dangling from its bill. The cries of the starving child redoubled, its dipping motion became a frantic tic. This is a continual rhythmic genuflection, and it is said that a dipper can "dip" as soon as it can stand. For one instant mother and child curtseyed to each other; then with a running flutter she rushed to him, crammed the food into his spread beak, and disappeared with the flying spray.

Surprisingly, the young one began to forage for himself. He turned over a twig, found another, found a titbit, swallowed it, waded a little into the stream, found another, and to my horror hopped right into the flume almost at the brink of this cataract ninety feet high! I ran along the parapet and looked down the fall for his mother. She was nowhere in sight. The spot where her youngster perched was slippery with algae; it was gusty with the down suction of the imminent plunge; the current was gathering momentum there like a millrace. My wife clapped her hands in terror; she called aloud to the child bird. He heard no voice to which he would respond, but waded out to his knees in the water, two inches from the brink. We clutched each other, parents both. But the happy birdling probed, got something, took another step, thought better of it, turned around, came back to the fir roots, and began playing a game that I suppose would be called "pick up sticks." You grasp a twig in your bill, shake it, think about it, drop it in the current, and find another one—if possible, a difficult bit of wood to extricate. This went on for many minutes. Sometimes, with luck, he found a caddis worm and gulped it. Unsure though his short wings still obviously were, he acted quite the worldling, as though long ago he had forgotten the nest. And yet it might have been this morning he had left it.

In the Yosemite I had seen that nest, a dome of moss carefully erected yet looking much as if it had been accidentally washed into that wedged position on a great boulder in midstream; the entrance is, uniquely, at the bottom, and I watched a dipper there come flying through the rapid waters for a little space and flick up and into the aperture bearing a worm for some invisible mouth within. That was the first time I had ever seen this bird, for I had just come out to the West. And in all of Chapman's *Handbook of Birds of Eastern North America* you will not find even the name. Other western birds turn up in the East—western meadowlarks on the prairies west of Chicago, marbled godwits south of it on the reedy lakes of the Calumet district, western willets on the Lake Michigan dunes. But never by any chance a dipper, for it cannot cross the great plains; it will not follow the muddy rivers; it has never been seen east of the Black Hills of South Dakota where the outposts of the western forests begin, with ponderosa and limber pines.

So dippers have never reached the Appalachian system, more's the pity. How they would love, I think, the terraced sheet of falling water in my Tryon glen! Or that other fall, the tall, wild, shouting one that plunges from the mountain of my childhood; I used to hear it, playing in the woods, before I knew they called it Shunkawakin.

Audubon himself never saw a dipper alive; he painted from specimens. Wilson did not know of it, I believe, to the day of his premature death. Major Long's expedition to the Rocky Mountains turned up no dipper, though surely the naturalist of the party would not have missed it had he seen it, for he was Thomas Say, discoverer of such new western birds as the cliff swallow and the linnet, the lazuli bunting and the rock wren and seven more. Warren's expedition to the headwaters of the Missouri and the Yellowstone brought back no word of it, and even Elliott Coues, stationed for years as an army surgeon in Dakota and in Arizona, never saw a dipper but once in all his life.

But long before eastern ornithologists had more than a few skins for their edification, and not a nest or an egg or any knowledge of either, beyond the continental wall dippers and men had made acquaintance. For this is a frank and cordial bird; not the fret of a mill nor the presence of man affrights him. And both the dippers and the Forty-Niners wanted something from the stream bottoms, so that many a bearded panner knew the liquid chittering song, while ornithologists of Boston and Philadelphia were writing "nidification unelucidated" and other dignified admissions of ignorance.

But since those days the ouzel has grown more retiring. Irrigation has stolen away his streams; pollution has disgusted him with them; deforestation has deprived him of his solitude. Yard by yard and mile by mile the dipper has lost ground, and territory he has abandoned he does not reclaim.

So that I knew that it was a fugitive bold beauty that I saw when the mother ouzel flashed back from the valley below. Up she came in a flight dark and silent as a bat's but with no such stagger; straight she came, graceful as a swallow but never gliding, beating her wings up, up, right into the glittering furious heart of the falls, up through the plunging water, to her eager child.

Be it set down, to my folly if you will, that in a world racked with war and worm-eaten with despair, I could somehow take an entire day and devote it to the doings of two dippers, and the dance of one slender cascade. I do not know how to justify my way of life, any more than I know how long it can continue. I can only say that this too is reality; this too is truth, this also is the business of a man, and its own wage.

THE FRASER

BRUCE HUTCHISON

Bruce Hutchison was born in 1901, in Prescott, Ontario, but grew up in British Columbia. In 1918, he began writing for the *Victoria Times*, and in 1944 became associate editor of the *Winnipeg Free Press*. Six years later he moved back to the *Times* as editor, and in 1963 became editorial director of the *Vancouver Sun* for which he wrote a weekly column until his death in 1992. Primarily a political reporter, he wrote biographies of several Canadian prime ministers but also short stories, a novel (*The Hollow Men*, 1944), and essays about Canadians and their connection with the land. His best-known books are *The Unknown Country: Canada and Her People* (1943) and *The Unfinished Country* (1985). He believed that it was the country's essentially rural values that made modern Canada a great nation. In 1950 he was chosen to write about British Columbia's Fraser River for Rinehart and Company's (formerly Farrar and Rinehart) Rivers of America series, and in this opening passage he matches the awesome spectacle of the river with his own considerable descriptive powers.

. . .

NO MAN STANDS beside the Fraser River without sensing the precarious hold of his species upon the earth. This fact is disclosed, perhaps, by all of nature's larger spectacles, but here it is thrust upon you with a special clarity. In this grisly trench, bored out of solid rock through unimaginable time by the scour of brown water, the long history of lifeless matter, the pitifully brief record of life, the mere moment of man's existence, are suddenly legible. And here, in this prodigal waste of energy, nature's war on all living creatures is naked, brutal and ceaseless.

Of all of America's great rivers the Fraser is probably the most unfriendly to mammalian life. The fish it tolerates and breeds in countless swarm. The vegetable growth it burrows out and sweeps away wherever its tides can reach. The animal touches these waters at its peril. Among the animals, the river has seen man for a fragment of time hardly worth recording in the ages of its experience and it holds him in contempt. It crushes his vessels. It tugs and chews forever at his bridges. It heaves its avalanches against his fragile railways. It gnaws his little plots of habitable land, overwhelms his dikes, silts up his harbours, and awaits the day of his going.

In the lash and spill of water, in the slow grinding of rock and cliff, in the perpetual slide of mountain and forest, in the erosion of mountain and gumbo rangeland, in the impact of whirlpool and winter ice, the river is forever mad, ravenous and lonely.

Like many other species which have lived beside it and disappeared, man, though he may build a few dams and tunnels, is a helpless spectator of this process. He cannot look upon it without knowing that he, too, will disappear in due time, he and all his kind, leaving only a few scratches on the shore. These the river will erase at leisure...

In shape it is an elongated letter S; in length 850 miles without its vast mesh of tributaries; in aspect ugly and sublime; in character violent and treacherous; in potential usefulness the largest source of electrical power left in North America.

Its first waters drip from the melting snows of the Rockies' central range, some three hundred miles north of the American border, latitude 25° 45', and hard by the upper reaches of the Columbia, which almost duplicates the Fraser's seaward journey farther to the south. The milky sweat of glaciers, the oozings of the mountain mosses, the clean upland puddles, and the tiny cataracts among the rock slides form the first creeks which, joining in a narrow lake, begin a leisurely and deceptive passage northwestward through British Columbia. Fresh from the snow and well-washed mountainsides, the little river is green and cleanly.

At the top of its northern arc the Fraser almost slips over the northern watershed of the continent. A few miles away, the first small members of the great Mackenzie family are beginning their long voyage to the Arctic. A minute tilt of land would join the Fraser to this northern flow, but the little elevation along the arc turns it southward. Thus barely escaping the pull of the arctic drainage basin, the Fraser, now a mighty river and growing with every mile, searches for a passage to the Pacific.

Between it and the ocean lie the several ranges of the Coast mountains, some of them higher than the Canadian Rockies.

For more than four hundred miles there is no direct opening through this barrier. The Fraser is forced to move southward across the broad inland plateau, where it easily digs for itself a yawning ditch through the yielding gumbo.

In the early stages its journey is monotonous. It moves among sombre hills, dark with forests of spruce and jack pine, and every mile is the same. By now it is gathering volume and speed. Its load of sediment has turned its water to the colour of pale treacle.

At its southward turn it absorbs its first great tributary, the Nechako, from the lake country to the west. Now its canyon is deepening and widening but at one famous danger point its current is suddenly compressed in a narrow gate of rock to spill over a few miles of rapids, where the skeletons of ancient ships and barges still lie across the sand bars. Having passed this first obstruction, the river is soon running free again.

Now it is swollen by the Quesnel, which it sucks in from the eastward. From the west it swallows the Chilcotin out of the coastal snow. It has left the timbered country and is cutting through an open rangeland of bunch grass and sagebrush.

It is still growing. Some hundred miles to the south it meets its only serious rival, the Thompson, whose northern branch has risen not far from the Fraser's own source in the Rockies but has moved down an eastern trench and then swung west through the Dry Belt.

At their junction the Thompson looks almost as large and tumultuous as the Fraser but is instantly engulfed in the main current with a gaudy blend of colour. Its leagues of clay have turned the Fraser to a deep and oily brown. The Thompson, cleansed by its filtering lakes to the eastward, is a hard blue-green. As it surges into the Fraser at Lytton the Thompson cuts a sharp line across the muddy substance of its parent, like a vein of precious metal on a bed of dull ore. The margin of this clean water is so fixed and solid that you can almost believe that the two rivers are made of different elements. But at the edge of this bubbling mixture the Thompson suddenly disappears.

The character of the Fraser has changed. Its direction is still south but it has collided for the first time with the Coast Range, which runs from the southeast to the northwest sideways along the edge of the continent. Seeking a pass to the sea, the current moves in a quickened pace but yet parallel to the coast. It is now squeezed tight within the mountains and turns furious at its imprisonment. Its channel here is cut out of the living rock, its trench dug ever deeper to accommodate its distended body, its water convulsed in whirlpool, back eddy and hidden cavern.

This is the black canyon of the Fraser, where even the salmon is often hurled bodily from the current, where the first explorers crawled on hands and knees along the edges of the precipice, where the Indians travelled on dangling ladders, where the gold rush hauled its freight by a road built on stilts, where the engineers blasted their railway grades out of the naked cliffs.

The canyon has been called beautiful. If this be beauty, it is the beauty of nightmare. It has been called magnificent, but this is the magnificence of destruction. It has been called sublime, and so it is, with the sublimity of blind and senseless force.

From the road, high up the mountains, the river appears as a twisted line of brown, solid and motionless, no wider than a clothesline. The Coast Range around it, unlike the more orderly defiles of the Rockies, sprawls in chaos as if its builders had mislaid their plans—a jumble of ragged peaks, dim gorges, smears of green forest, shadows miles wide in ceaseless shift of pattern.

Hour by hour this jumble of rock, earth, timber and water changes its aspect and almost seems to change its substance in men's sight. At dawn the surface of the mountains thrusts itself out, acquires body and shape and seems to lurch toward the river. At noon, as the shadows move down them, the slopes retreat, fading into dull greys and greens. In the twilight the canyon is hung with ragged curtains of blue and purple, haze streams out of every crevice and the mountains stand solid against the stars, almost within touch of your hand. Always, in daylight or dark, the canyon is clamorous with the voice of its passenger.

In such a closed and wrinkled pocket man and his works are lost. The two railways and the single road have left only a nick on the cliffs, a few feet of level space across the slides. A freight train a mile long is a toiling worm, at night a glow worm, whose spark flickers for a moment and is snuffed out. Only a wink of light from some railway town on the canyon's lip proclaims the presence of any life but the river's.

To observe the dimensions and power of this larger life you must crawl down the rock slides to the riverbank. There the smooth line of water as seen from the mountains turns into a paroxysm of dirty foam, rising and falling in steady pulse. The perpetual mist has coated the canyon walls with slime and the water has worn them smooth, squared them off like old masonry so that in places they might have been built by human hands. A few islands still stand in the channel, whittled down to narrow splinters and already doomed. The final product of this erosion, the white sand pulverized out of the mountainsides, is laid in glistening bars by every back eddy. The dust of gold lies in these bars from the undiscovered mother lode.

All other sounds, the human voice, the whistle of the locomotive a few yards off, are obliterated by the din of this cauldron. The motion of the river seems to set the entire canyon in motion. Before the spectacle of flux, the beholder turns dizzy and, looking up, finds the cliffs closing over his head.

The river is larger than it appears. At the gut of Hell's Gate, where it finally breaches the central spine of the mountains, it is only 120 feet wide, but its constricted body has bored a channel for itself 85 feet deep at low water and as deep as 175 feet in summer freshet. It moves here sometimes at the rate of 20 feet a second, too fast even for the passage of salmon.

At last the river has found its outlet to the sea. At Hope it bursts out of the canyon, turns straight west, and pours down the coastal shelf.

Now the character of the river country changes again. Moving in from the Pacific, the clouds have collided with the mountains and dumped their rain on the western slope to nourish the Pacific jungle. The sparse, red-barked pine, the jack pine, the flat juniper and shivering poplar, which have followed the river through the Dry Belt, give way to close-packed fir, hemlock, balsam, maple and alder. After the bare clay of sagebrush and tumbleweed, the ground is rank with fern, salal and devil's club. All at once, in hardly more than a mile, the river emerges from the mountains and the jungle to find itself ample elbowroom in a lush and open valley.

On the silt dumped by the current before he appeared man now grows his crops and feeds his dairy herds. Still the river is not to be trusted. It continually threatens and often overflows the dikes he has built against it. But after the madness of its youth it spends its last years in relative peace. Toward its mouth it tolerates the ships of remote oceans, the tugs and log booms of commerce, and the white flocks of sea gulls feeding on its refuse. Thus past the busy port of New Westminster, across the delta of its own making, by three separate channels heavy with its silt, this weariest river moves somehow safe to sea.

The journey has been long and laborious. The Fraser has travelled nearly a thousand miles. It has drained two mountain ranges and 91,000 square miles of land, more than the area of many great nations, nearly twice the entire space of New York State, nearly one and a half times the size of Washington. It has laid the alluvial site and by its commerce has built the world port of Vancouver. Its power has lighted this city and propelled most of Canada's industry west of the Rockies. Its waters have irrigated a hundred thousand acres. Its silt has provided some of the most fertile farm land in the world. It has altered the course of man's life in America. Even on the sea it has left its indelible mark, a gout of brown smeared for miles across the green salt waters, as if the Fraser were loath to die.

THE BIG
BLACKFOOT

NORMAN MACLEAN

Norman Maclean was a native of Clarinda, Iowa, the son of a Scottish Presbyterian minister and ardent outdoorsman. In 1909 the family moved to Missoula, Montana, and Maclean and his brother, Paul, took up fly-fishing in earnest. Maclean graduated from Dartmouth College in 1924 and the University of Chicago in 1928, and he remained there as a professor of English until his retirement in 1973. It was then he began writing. *A River Runs Through It*, from which this excerpt is taken, appeared in 1976—the first book of fiction ever published by the University of Chicago Press, although there is nothing fictional about this fast-paced, semi-autobiographical description of Montana's Big Blackfoot River. Maclean's only other book, *Young Men and Fire*, appeared posthumously in 1992.

. . .

PAUL AND I FISHED a good many big rivers, but when one of us referred to "the big river" the other knew it was the Big Blackfoot. It isn't the biggest river we fished, but it is the most powerful, and per pound, so are its fish. It runs straight and hard—on a map or from an airplane it is almost a straight line running due west from its headwaters at Rogers Pass on the Continental Divide to Bonner, Montana, where it empties into the South Fork of the Clark Fork of the Columbia. It runs hard all the way.

Near its headwaters on the Continental Divide there is a mine with a thermometer that stopped at 69.7 degrees below zero, the lowest temperature ever officially recorded in the United States (Alaska omitted). From its headwaters to its mouth it was manufactured by glaciers. The first sixty-five miles of it are smashed against the southern wall of its valley by glaciers that moved in from the north, scarifying the earth; its lower twenty-five miles were made overnight when the great glacial lake covering northwestern Montana and northern Idaho broke its ice dam and spread the remains of Montana and Idaho mountains over hundreds of miles of the plains of eastern Washington. It was the biggest flood in the world for which there is geological evidence; it was so vast a geological event that the mind of man could only conceive of it but could not prove it until photographs could be taken from earth satellites.

The straight line on the map also suggests its glacial origins; it has no meandering valley, and its few farms are mostly on its southern tributaries which were not ripped up by glaciers; instead of opening into a wide flood plain near its mouth, the valley, which was cut overnight by a disappearing lake when the great ice dam melted, gets narrower and narrower until the only way a river, an old logging railroad, and an automobile road can fit into it is for two of them to take to the mountainsides.

It is a tough place for a trout to live—the river roars and the water is too fast to let algae grow on the rocks for feed, so there is no fat on the fish, which must hold most trout records for high jumping.

Besides, it is the river we knew best. My brother and I had fished the Big Blackfoot since nearly the beginning of the century—my father before then. We regarded it as a family river, as a part of us, and I surrender it now only with great reluctance to dude ranches, the unselected inhabitants of Great Falls, and the Moorish invaders from California...

The canyon above the old Clearwater bridge is where the Blackfoot roars loudest. The backbone of a mountain would not break, so the mountain compresses the already powerful river into sound and spray before letting it pass. Here, of course, the road leaves the river; there was no place in the canyon for an Indian trail; even in 1806 when Lewis left Clark to come up the Blackfoot, he skirted the canyon by a safe margin. It is no place for small fish or small fishermen. Even the roar adds power to the fish or at least intimidates the fisherman.

When we fished the canyon we fished on the same side of it for the simple reason that there is no place in the canyon to wade across. I could hear Paul start to pass me to get to the hole above, and, when I realized I didn't hear him anymore, I knew he had stopped to watch me. Although I have never pretended to be a great fisherman, it was always important to me that I was a fisherman and looked like one, especially when fishing with my brother. Even before the silence continued, I knew that I wasn't looking like much of anything.

Although I have a warm personal feeling for the canyon, it is not an ideal place for me to fish. It puts a premium upon being able to cast for distance, and yet most of the time there are cliffs or trees right behind the fisherman so he has to keep all his line in front of him. It's like a baseball pitcher being deprived of his windup, and it forces the fly fisherman into what is called a "roll cast," a hard cast that I have never mastered. The fisherman has to work enough line into his cast to get distance without throwing any line behind him, and then he has to develop enough power from a short arc to shoot it out across the water.

He starts accumulating the extra amount of line for the long cast by retrieving his last cast so slowly that an unusual amount of line stays in the water and what is out of it forms a slack semi-loop. The loop is enlarged by raising the casting arm straight up and cocking the wrist until it points to 1:30. There, then, is a lot of line in front of the fisherman, but it takes about everything he has to get it high in the air and out over the water so that the fly and leader settle ahead of the line—the arm is a piston, the wrist is a revolver that uncocks, and even the body gets behind the punch. Important, too, is the fact that the extra amount of line remaining in the water until the last moment gives a semisolid bottom to the cast. It is a little like a rattlesnake striking, with a good piece of his tail on the ground as something to strike from. All this is easy for a rattlesnake, but has always been hard for me.

Paul knew how I felt about my fishing and was careful not to seem superior by offering advice, but he had watched so long that he couldn't leave now without saying something. Finally he said, "The fish are out farther." Probably fearing he had put a strain on family relations, he quickly added, "Just a little farther."

I reeled in my line slowly, not looking behind so as not to see him. Maybe he was sorry he had spoken, but, having said what he said, he had to say something more. "Instead of retrieving the line straight toward you, bring it in on a diagonal from the downstream side. The diagonal will give you a more resistant base to your loop so you can put more power into your forward cast and get a little more distance."

Then he acted as if he hadn't said anything and I acted as if I hadn't heard it, but as soon as he left, which was immediately, I started retrieving my line on a diagonal, and it helped. The moment I felt I was getting a little more distance I ran for a fresh hole to make a fresh start in life.

It was a beautiful stretch of water, either to a fisherman or a photographer, although each would have focused his equipment on a different point. It was a barely submerged waterfall. The reef of rock was about two feet under the water, so the whole river rose into one wave, shook itself into spray, then fell back on itself and turned blue. After it recovered from the shock, it came back to see how it had fallen.

No fish could live out there where the river exploded into the colors and curves that would attract photographers. The fish were in that slow backwash, right in the dirty foam, with the dirt being one of the chief attractions. Part of the speckles would be pollen from pine trees, but most of the dirt was edible insect life that had not survived the waterfall.

I studied the situation. Although maybe I had just added three feet to my roll cast, I still had to do a lot of thinking before casting to compensate for some of my other shortcomings. But I felt I had already made the right beginning—I had already figured out where the big fish would be and why.

Then an odd thing happened. I saw him. A black back rose and sank in the foam. In fact, I imagined I saw spines on his dorsal fin until I said to myself, "God, he couldn't be so big you could see his fins." I even added, "You wouldn't even have seen the fish in all that foam if you hadn't first thought he would be there." But I couldn't shake the conviction that I had seen the black back of a big fish, because, as someone often forced to think, I know that often I would not see a thing unless I thought of it first.

Seeing the fish that I first thought would be there led me to wondering which way he would be pointing in the river. "Remember, when you make the first cast," I thought, "that you saw him in the backwash where the water is circling upstream, so he will be looking downstream, not upstream, as he would be if he were in the main current."

I was led by association to the question of what fly I would cast, and to the conclusion that it had better be a large fly, a number four or six, if I was going after the big hump in the foam.

From the fly, I went to the other end of the cast, and asked myself where the hell I was going to cast from. There were only gigantic rocks at this waterfall, so I picked one of the biggest, saw how I could crawl up it, and knew from that added height I would get added distance, but then I had to ask myself, "How the hell am I going to land the fish if I hook him while I'm standing up there?" So I had to pick a smaller rock, which would shorten my distance but would let me slide down it with a rod in my hand and a big fish on.

I was gradually approaching the question all river fishermen should ask before they make the first cast, "If I hook a big one, where the hell can I land him?"

One great thing about fly fishing is that after a while nothing exists of the world but thoughts about fly fishing. It is also interesting that thoughts about fishing are often carried on in dialogue form where Hope and Fear—or, many times, two Fears—try to outweigh each other.

One Fear looked down the shoreline and said to me (a third person distinct from the two fears), "There is nothing but rocks for thirty yards, but don't get scared and try to land him before you get all the way down to the first sandbar."

The Second Fear said, "It's forty, not thirty, yards to the first sandbar and the weather has been warm and the fish's mouth will be soft and he will work off the hook if you try to fight him forty yards downriver. It's not good but it will be best to try to land him on a rock that is closer."

The First Fear said, "There is a big rock in the river that you will have to take him past before you land him, but, if you hold the line tight enough on him to keep him this side of the rock, you will probably lose him."

The Second Fear said, "But if you let him get on the far side of the rock, the line will get caught under it, and you will be sure to lose him."

That's how you know when you have thought too much—when you become a dialogue between *You'll probably lose* and *You're sure to lose*. But I didn't entirely quit thinking, although I did switch subjects. It is not in the book yet it is human enough to spend a moment before casting in trying to imagine what the fish is thinking, even if one of its eggs is as big as its brain and even if, when you swim underwater, it is hard to imagine that a fish has anything to think about. Still, I could never be talked into believing that all a fish knows is hunger and fear. I have tried to feel nothing but hunger and fear and don't see how a fish could ever grow to six inches if that were all he ever felt. In fact, I go so far sometimes as to imagine that a fish thinks pretty thoughts. Before I made the cast, I imagined the fish with the black back lying cool in the carbonated water full of bubbles from the waterfalls. He was looking downriver and watching the foam with food in it backing upstream like a floating cafeteria coming to wait on its customers. And he probably was imagining that the speckled foam was eggnog with nutmeg sprinkled on it, and, when the whites of eggs separated and he saw what was on shore, he probably said to himself, "What a lucky son of a bitch I am that this guy and not his brother is about to fish this hole."

I thought all these thoughts and some besides that proved of no value, and then I cast and I caught him.

AWASH
IN THE BALEH

REDMOND O'HANLON

British travel writer Redmond O'Hanlon studied English at Oxford University and for fifteen years was the natural history editor for the *Times Literary Supplement*. His first book, published in 1984, was about the influence of Darwin and scientific thought on the novels of Joseph Conrad, but since then all his writing has been about bizarre quests in exotic locales. *Into the Heart of Borneo*, excerpted here, also published in 1984, is about a trip he took to Borneo with the poet James Fenton and a troupe of Iban guides to search for the possibly mythical Borneo rhinoceros. He has documented similarly arduous and hilarious pseudo expeditions in *In Trouble Again* (1988), *No Mercy: A Journey into the Heart of the Congo* (1997), and his most recent book, *Trawler* (2005). O'Hanlon lives near Oxford.

．　．　．

THE RIVER TWISTED and turned and grew narrower and the great creepers, tumbling down in profusion from two hundred feet above our heads, edged closer. Every now and then

95

we would pass a tangle of river-rubbish, leaves and sticks and dead ferns, seemingly caught in the lianas by floodwater some forty feet above the present water-level. So why did the high banks not show more sign of recent devastation? Idly watching one such clump as Leon arced the boat close to the bank before making a run up a rapid, we solved the mystery. A dumpy bird, thrush-sized, its blue and yellow beak framed by whiskers, black on its back, scarlet on its stomach, popped out of a side opening: the suspended bunches of debris were the nests of the Black-and-red broadbill.

The rapids and cascades became more frequent. We had to jump out into the river more often, sometimes to our waists, sometimes to our armpits, guiding the dugout into a side channel away from the main crash of the water through the central rocks, pushing it up the shallows.

"Saytu, dua, tiga—bata!" sang Dana, which even we could reconstruct as one, two, three, and push.

The Iban gripped the round, algae-covered stones on the river-bed easily with their muscled, calloused, spatulate toes. Our boots slipped into crevices, slithered away in the current, threatened to break off a leg at the ankle or the knee. It was only really possible to push hard when the boat was still, stuck fast, and then Headmaster Dana would shout "Badas!" "Well done!" But the most welcome cry became "Npan! Npan!", an invitation to get back in, quick.

Crossing one such deep pool, collapsed in the boat, the engine re-started, we found ourselves staring at a gigantic

Bearded pig sitting quietly on his haunches on the bank. Completely white, an old and lonely male, he looked at us with his piggy eyes. Dana, throwing his pole into the boat, snatched up his shotgun; Leon, abandoning the rudder, followed suit. Inghai shouted a warning, the canoe veered sideways into the current, the shotguns were discarded, the boat re-aligned, and the pig, no longer curious, ambled off into the jungle, his enormous testicles swaying along behind him.

We entered a wide reach of foaming water. The choppy waves, snatching this way and that, had ripped caves of soil out of the banks, leaving hundreds of yards of overhang on either side. There was an ominous noise of arguing currents ahead. The rapids-preamble, the white water, the moving whirlpools, the noise ahead, was longer and louder than it ought to have been.

With the canoe pitching feverishly, we rounded a sweeping bend; and the reason for the agitated river, the unaccustomed roar, became obvious. The Green Heave ahead was very much higher than any we had met. There was a waterfall to the left of the river-course, a huge surging of water over a ledge, with the way to the right blocked by thrown-up trees, piles of roots dislodged upstream, torn out in floods, and tossed aside here against a line of rocks. There was, however, one small channel through, a shallow rapid, dangerously close to the main rush of water, but negotiable, separated from the torrent by three huge boulders.

Keeping well clear of the great whirlpool beneath the waterfall, Leon, guided between rocks by Inghai's semaphore-like gestures, brought the boat to the base of this normal-size rapid. Dana, James and I made our way carefully up with the bow-rope, whilst Leon and Inghai held the dugout steady.

Dana held the lead position on the rope; I stood behind him and James behind me. We pulled, Leon and Inghai pushed. The boat moved up and forward some fifteen feet and then stuck. Leon and Inghai walked up the rapid, kneeling, hunching and shoving, rolling small rocks aside to clear a channel. We waited on the lip of the rock above, pulling on the rope to keep the longboat straight, to stop it rolling sideways, tiring in the push of water round our waists. At last Leon and Inghai were ready. But the channel they had had to make was a little to our right as we looked down at them, a little to their left, a little closer to the waterfall. To pull straight we must move to our right. Dana pointed to our new positions.

It was only a stride or two. But the level of the river-bed suddenly dipped, long since scooped away by the pull of the main current. James lost his footing, and, trying to save himself, let go of the rope. I stepped back and across to catch him, the rope bound round my left wrist, snatching his left hand in my right. His legs thudded into mine, tangled, and then swung free, into the current, weightless, as if a part of him had been knocked into outer space. His hat came off, hurtled past his shoes, spun in an eddy, and disappeared over the lip of the fall.

His fingers were very white; and slippery. He bites his fingernails; and they could not dig into my palm. He simply looked surprised; his head seemed a long way from me. He was feeling underwater with his free arm, impossibly trying to grip a boulder with his other hand, to get a purchase on a smooth and slimy rock, a rock polished smooth, for centuries, by perpetual tons of rolling water.

His fingers bent straighter, slowly edging out of mine, for hour upon hour, or so it felt, but it must have been in seconds. His arm rigid, his fingertips squeezed out of my fist. He turned in the current, spread-eagled. Still turning, but much faster, he was sucked under; his right ankle and shoe were bizarrely visible above the surface; he was lifted slightly, a bundle of clothes, of no discernible shape, and then he was gone.

"Boat! Boat!" shouted Dana, dropping the rope, bounding down the rocks of the side rapid, crouched, using his arms like a baboon.

"Hold the boat! Hold the boat!" yelled Leon.

James's bald head, white and fragile as an owl's egg, was sweeping round in the whirlpool below, spinning, bobbing up and down in the foaming water, each orbit of the current carrying him within inches of the black rocks at its edge.

Leon jumped into the boat, clambered on to the raised outboard-motor frame, squatted, and then, with a long, yodelling cry, launched himself in a great curving leap into the centre of the maelstrom. He disappeared, surfaced, shook his head, spotted James, dived again, and caught him. Inghai, too, was in the water, but, closing with them for a moment, he faltered, was overwhelmed, and swept downstream. Leon, holding on to James, made a circuit of the whirlpool until, reaching the exit current, he thrust out like a turtle and they followed Inghai downriver, edging, yard by yard, towards the bank.

Obeying Dana's every sign, I helped him coax the boat on to a strip of shingle beneath the dam of logs. James, when we walked down to him, was sitting on a boulder. Leon sat beside him, an arm around his shoulders.

"You be all right soon, my friend," said Leon "you be all right soon, my very best friend. Soon you be so happy."

James, bedraggled, looking very sick, his white lips an open O in his black beard, was hyper-ventilating dangerously, taking great rhythmic draughts of oxygen, his body shaking.

"You be okay," said Leon. "I not let you die my old friend."

Just then little Inghai appeared, beaming with pride, holding aloft one very wet straw boater.

"I save hat!" said Inghai, "Jams! Jams! I save hat!"

James looked up, smiled, and so stopped his terrible spasms of breathing. He really was going to be all right.

Suddenly, it all seemed funny, hilariously funny. "Inghai saved his hat!" We laughed and laughed, rolling about on the shingle. "Inghai saved his hat! Ingy-pingy saved his hat!" It was, I am ashamed to say, the first (and I hope it will be the last) fit of genuine medically-certifiable hysterics which I have ever had.

THE RIVER

RODERICK HAIG-BROWN

Roderick Langmere Haig-Brown was truly a Renaissance man. Born in Sussex, England, in 1908—his father was schoolmaster of Lancing College and his godfather was Lord Baden-Powell—he trained as a lawyer, worked as a logger and cougar hunter, and eventually became a judge in Campbell River, British Columbia, his home for many decades. Shortly before Haig-Brown's death in 1976, the poet Al Purdy described him as "a medium-sized, brown-faced, balding man... quiet with the stillness of natural things" and as "a literary fisherman." He wrote twenty-five books, most of them about rivers and fishing, which, as he explains in this excerpt from *Measure of the Year* (1950), he often found inseparable.

. . .

I SHOULD LIKE TO have many houses beside many rivers, except that a man can only live in one house at a time. If he had many houses by many rivers he would always be regretting the houses left empty and the rivers unwatched.

Perhaps I have had my share of waking and sleeping beside different rivers. Grandfather's house stood on the banks of one clear running little Dorset stream and another larger stream was only two or three hundred yards away across the fields. For years I lived in logging camps, most of them overlooking lakes or streams, or else made my own camp nightly beside whatever stream was nearest. Through part of two winters I ran trap lines from a cabin set in the fork of a river that drained a timbered valley. Even in London I managed to rent one room within sight of the Thames, and another as near, though turned from it.

Now Ann and I have lived sixteen years within sight and sound of the Elk and seem likely to live here another sixteen or sixty years. It should be enough. Yet not so long ago I bid on a four-hundred-acre island lying in the mouth of a northern river; the island was listed in a tax sale and my bid didn't take it because the owner reclaimed, but my intention was definite enough. From time to time Ann and I idly explore the next large river valley north of us, searching always for some place above flood level that commands a good stretch of the river, upstream and down. And well south of here, along the highway to Victoria, one comes suddenly upon a tiny white church built among great maple trees at the entrance to a narrow bridge on a sharp curve. On the far side of the bridge is a red-roofed frame house set well down on a flat between the river and an old grass-grown bed that is dry except in floodtime. The little river is slow and clear and deep near the house, with an easy sloping bank on which there is nearly always an upturned canoe or rowboat. Upstream, at a bend, there is the half-hidden stir of a little rapid. I never pass that house without wanting to live there for a spell. Yet I know the river can flood and I suspect the house is set too well down, too comfortably beside the river's workaday level to be safe in flood.

I cannot altogether separate this obsession with rivers from the lore and habit of fishing and hunting, yet I think it is a natural thing for a man to love a river, and I think I should still want to live by one if I had never caught a fish or fired a gun. A river is life and light, especially in timbered country; it is always the easiest natural way of travel and it is used as such by many creatures besides man. No clean river can be other than beautiful and it has changing beauty. Even a streamlet can become impressive in floodtime and the greatest of rivers has a light, almost intimate quality of gentleness at its lowest summer level.

The Elk is not a big river. It flows at an average of twenty-three hundred cubic feet a second throughout the year, at thirty thousand cubic feet in extreme freshet, and about four hundred cubic feet in its quietest moments. This last figure works out at about a hundred and fifty thousand gallons a minute, while the extreme freshet figure means something over eleven million gallons a minute; even in gallons and minutes the figures don't mean as much as they should, but here at the house that freshet figure is an awe-inspiring quantity of water going by very, very fast, so fast that every rock on the bottom throws a pattern on the surface and the bigger rocks break white water even when they are five or six feet under. The summer figure is a rippling flow so easy and gentle that I can pole the big canoe quite easily against the very center of the steep little rapid just above the house.

The Elk follows a pattern fairly common in the short mountainous streams of the coast. At its mouth there was once a flat tidal meadow, less than a mile square, shielded by a long sandspit and beloved by ducks and geese and swans. A big logging company's booming ground has long since chased the geese and most of the ducks away, dredging and pile-driving have changed the channels and hidden the meadow, but it is still a lovely place, made alive by the tidal changes and the many creatures that tolerate human activity and settlement. Ospreys hunt there and herons wait. Kildeer and yellowlegs and many sandpipers are there in spring; meadowlarks sing from the fence posts, grebes and mergansers nest in the slough, loons fish in the channel, mink and coon hunt the shorelines, an occasional bear comes down through the farms, cormorants perch on the piles, Bonaparte's gulls flock in to rest on the log booms.

Only a mile or two above tidewater the river is enclosed in a high, narrow canyon of rock, which it enters through a lovely fall of well over a hundred feet. The fall has always controlled the river's character, changing it sharply from a coastal stream with runs of salmon and all the other anadromous fish to a landlocked watershed; limiting its usefulness to canoe travelers and turning them away to trails and roads. And now at last it has meant power, the first dam above the falls, the big dam just below the first lake, the powerhouse at the foot of the canyon.

The first two big lakes take the river's name, Upper and Lower Elk Lake, but above the upper lake the river loses its own name in the name of the third and largest lake of its chain and becomes Strathcona River. This is always happening to rivers, sometimes without any logical break such as a lake to make it happen, and it serves a useful purpose in closely identifying the different reaches. But merely changing a name cannot make a river tributary to itself; it has always a true headwater, an ultimate source in spring or snowbank or glacier, whence it comes to gather its tributaries into its single purposeful bed that follows always the lowest floor of its valley to the sea. Our river rises in summer snow on the slopes of the high mountains to the south of Strathcona Lake, gathers the tiny streams from other slopes and peaks until it is a sizable creek, joins another creek almost as large as itself, and comes coldly and quietly into the big lake through a tangled flat where elk and beaver work.

For twenty miles from there the lake is the river's bed and along both sides of the lake are high mountains, five and six and seven thousand feet high, cut by short deep valleys that bring more water from snow fields and little lakes. In the length of the lake the river takes to itself seven major tributaries, each one from a valley of untouched timber, and a hundred lesser streams; as it leaves the lake it is full river size, broad and fine, and it takes another valley's river to itself just before it enters the upper lake.

I call the river mine, without owning any foot of it from source to sea and without any thought of possession in the ordinary sense. At one time or another I have walked most of the valley's length; I have traveled a good part of it by boat and canoe; I have waded most places where wading is possible and the fishing makes it worthwhile. I have blazed trees at the level of highest flood and have studied the depressions and hidden rocks of the bottom in lowest summer water. I know the rhythms of the salmon and trout runs of the length below the falls and something of the landlocked fish above the falls. I know where to expect beaver and elk and deer and bear and cougar. I know what ducks I shall see in summertime, where the geese and swans will find open water in freeze-up. I can name at least some of the May flies and stone flies and sedges that live out their lives along the river. I know the trees of its valley and some of the rock formations; I know the temperature of the mountain streams that feed it and the variations of temperature in the river itself when it has passed through the lakes. I can remember other years and recognize changes and make pronouncements that sound wise even to myself. In all this there is an intimacy akin to possession and far more important than possession. I do not want possession, only freedom of the river; and with every growth of knowledge and experience freedom grows.

Because I have learned so much of the river through fishing and watching fish, it is difficult to write of it without thinking of fish. From a fisherman's point of view almost everything about a river is related to fish and fishing. Floods or drought may mean disaster to spawning and hatch, or merely disappointed hopes of good fishing; birds and animals that live along the banks are predators or controls or both; insect life, in the water and out if it, is feed; lime content, temperature, weed growth, log jams, shallows or deeps, all have meaning in terms of fish and fishing. Even trees and brush overhanging the banks, even the work of beavers and muskrats, has bearing. It may seem a narrow view, but the interrelationships are so far reaching and complicated that it is really comprehensive; if anything is not included, the fisherman is almost certain to include it because observation is one of the keenest pleasures of his sport. A deer seen by the waterside, a yellowthroat's nest at the edge of a lake, the burst of dogwood blossoms along the banks in springtime, the curve of sunlit water over a smooth rock, all these things are important to his sport as the fish themselves, and he does not pass them by.

But for the accident of the falls, the Elk would be an even finer salmon river than it is; the streams above the lakes would have supported the spawning of thousands upon thousands of sockeye salmon and the lakes themselves would have raised the young fish through the year or two they spend in freshwater before migration. As it is, the Elk itself has only a mile or two of good spawning water and only one important tributary that the salmon can reach. In spite of this the river supports one of the most famous runs of big spring salmon in the world, as well as significant runs of two other salmon and two species of trout. The cycle of these runs, spawning, hatching of fry, growth of young fish, migration, and return, make much of the character of the lower river. It is on these, in the last analysis, that eagles and mergansers, ospreys and mallards and goldeneye, coon and mink and bear and otter depend, as does an important part of Elkhorn's population.

And the runs themselves, although the river is closed off above the falls, depend not only on this short two miles of breeding water, but upon the river's whole system. The stored snow under the virgin timber in the headwaters is the first resource; cut away the timber and much of it would be wasted, run off in times when the lower river did not need it. The delaying storage of the lakes is important, as is their power to settle silt of flood, to mingle temperatures and hold them low in storage; for silt chokes spawning beds, and high temperatures speed hatching times, low temperatures delay them too long. The aeration of all the rapids and falls above the lakes, perhaps that of the big falls themselves, is important to the fish and all life that feeds them. These things add up to the real river, a good strong flow of clear, clean water over a broad and rocky bed, rarely too strong, rarely too feeble, rarely too warm or too cold. They add up also, especially the lakes and the protecting timber of the hills, to the river's hundred and fifty thousand horsepower of electricity. And they are the country's beauty. It will be a foolish and criminal hand that interferes farther with them...

If one had to live out a life whose sight was limited to the breadth of the river at one place, the full measure of the year and all the seasons would be in it, as plainly there as in the pages of the handsomest calendar ever drawn. It would be a record of contrasts and mergence: the slow moving black water of January's binding cold against the sunlit rush of melting snow in the heat of June; revealing shallowness of August, with brown and green algae on the rocks, wiped utterly away in November's bank-high torrent; March rains building the flow in murky haste, to settle into the cleaner, still growing run-off of April and May; September's hesitancy, broken by the spawning salmon, becoming October of the drowned and drifting leaves and the dying fish. One could watch and call the winter's weight and spring's delay from hold of fullness in July, look out and know how November winds had blown from the river's height in early December.

We live with the river and seldom forget it for long, but we are not always sharply conscious of it. The stranger hears its sound as he lies in bed waiting for sleep; we do not, unless we listen for it. For days on end we may scarcely think of the river, letting its weight and volume leap and slide away "unheeded as a threshold book" in patterned flow towards the bridge and sea. This could be ungrateful failure, but I consider it rather a secure familiarity that takes much for granted between whiles. Except for the river we should not be here, living and growing as a family on this particular soil. Without the river there would be no sense in the way the windows look out from the house, the way the lawn runs and the trees are planted. Most of our days would be in some way different. And four different children than these would go out into the world, with different measures for their years.

THE HAWKESBURY

KATE GRENVILLE

Australian novelist Kate Grenville was born in Sydney in 1950, attended the University of Sydney, and has since lived in Britain, France, and the United States. She received a master's degree in creative writing from the University of Colorado in 1982 and has worked as a documentary filmmaker, journalist, and teacher. Her first novel, *Bearded Ladies,* appeared in 1984, the year after she returned to Australia; *Lilian's Story* (1985) won the Australian/Vogel Award; and *The Idea of Perfection* (2001) won the Orange Prize. The following haunting description of the Hawkesbury River, which flows into Broken Harbour just north of Sydney, Australia, is taken from her most recent novel, *The Secret River* (2005), an epic work that encompasses the founding of Sydney in the nineteenth century and that was nominated for the Man Booker Prize. The character of Thornhill, who first settles the region, is loosely based on Grenville's great-grandfather; "they" are the aboriginal inhabitants of the surrounding forests. Grenville lives in Sydney with her husband and two children.

.   .   .

THEN THEY WERE THROUGH. The sea was still churning and seething beneath the boat, but the wind was muted by land on all sides. They had pushed through into another geography altogether.

They call this Broken Bay, Blackwood said. *River comes in yonder.* He pointed ahead, where Thornhill could see only confusing stretches of water and thickly forested headlands. *Best hidden river in the world,* Blackwood said with satisfaction. *Never find your way in nor you'd been shown like I'm showing you.*

Looking inland, where gusts of wind scraped at the water, Thornhill strained to find that secret river. In every direction, the reaches of Broken Bay seemed to end in yet another wall of rock and forest. A man could sail around for days and never find his way into the Hawkesbury.

Blackwood pointed the boat towards a solid wall of land, a heaped-up ridge that tumbled down into the water all cliffs and skinny trees that grew out of the very stones themselves, and what had seemed a dead end slyly opened up into a stretch of river between cliffs. As the boat glided along on the tide, the cliffs rose sheer on both sides, mouse-grey except where the wind had exposed buttery rock, as if the landscape itself was a dark-skinned creature with golden flesh beneath.

The rock had been laid down flat, layer after layer piled high like flitches of timber. As it had worn away, great slabs the size of a house had fallen off and tumbled all skewiff at the foot of the cliffs. Some lay half in the water, melting away. Where the cliff met the water a tangle of snake-like roots, vines and mangroves knotted around the fallen boulders.

This was a place out of a dream, a fierce landscape of chasms and glowering cliffs and a vast unpredictable sky. Everywhere was the same but everywhere was different. Thornhill felt his eyes wide open, straining to find something they could understand.

It seemed the emptiest place in the world, too wild for any man to have made it his home. Then Blackwood said, *See yonder?* and pointed with his blunt hand at a promontory to port. Beyond the fringe of mangroves Thornhill could see tussocky grass and trees, and a heap of something pale. *Oysters, the shells,* Blackwood said, and watched the promontory fall behind them. *Suck the guts out, chuck the shells away. Been doing it since the year dot.* He laughed. *And fish! My word they get the fish.*

Not putting none by? Thornhill said. *For tomorrow, like?* Blackwood gave him an amused look. *Aye,* he said. *Not putting none by.* He slapped at a mosquito on his arm. *Why would they? River ain't going nowhere.*

WE START UP
THE GREAT MISSOURI

WILLIAM LEAST HEAT-MOON

William Least Heat-Moon was born William Trogdon, a descendant of a Lancastershire grandfather and a grandmother who was Osage, a member of the Sioux Nation. He served in the United States Navy, then set out in a truck to travel all the secondary highways in the United States, making a circle back to his Missouri home. His book about the odyssey, *Blue Highways: A Journey Into America* (1982), instantly identified Heat-Moon as one of the premier travel/nature writers of his generation. *PrairyErth: A Deep Map*, an ecological examination of Chase County, Kansas, appeared in 1991, and *River-Horse: The Logbook of a Boat Across America*, from which this description of his initial encounter with the Missouri River is taken, appeared in 1999. For that trip, Heat-Moon and seven shipmates—who are given the collective name Pilotis in the text—travelled from the Hudson River to the Columbia on a twenty-two-foot C-Dory motorboat named *Nikawa*, which in Osage means River-Horse. Heat-Moon lives near Columbia, Missouri, on the Missouri River.

. . .

WE HEARD THAT RAIN was coming down along the Missouri Valley out of eastern Kansas, causing the river to continue to rise, perhaps higher than the record flood of 1993, the most costly American alluvion ever. By departure time, a lone piece of good news—but an important one—suggested our route over the Great Plains at least should be well watered.

We pumped nearly four inches of rain out of the afterdeck, tightened down the canopy and kayak, set out onto the Mississippi, and headed toward the landing where began St. Louis, obscured that day in a rise of vapors, and on beyond the high Arch, the symbol of the city and the Missouri as Gateway to the West. Passing tows tore up the water, and *Nikawa* went into a violet rocking—pitching, yawing, rolling all at once—a varied chaos even Lake Erie had not worked upon us. We dodged drift and barges, jangled ourselves north through the hullabaloo morning, passed under the great Eads Bridge of 1874, a piece of engineering above all others that made St. Louis what it is. To the northwest on the Missouri ridge of Bellefontaine, "beautiful fountain," sleep the bones of William Clark; had they eyes, they could look across the river toward the place where the great Expedition began. We reached quiet water behind Gabaret Island on the dug channel that leads to the Chain-of-Rocks Lock, the final—or first—on the Mississippi and our last one for almost three thousand miles...

We returned to the Mississippi a little below the mouth of Wood River from where the Lewis and Clark Expedition embarked in 1804 on another day in May of similar wet and cheerless weather. We crossed the Mississippi, and there before us opened the great Missouri charging down fiercely a flood that bulled into the other river, hit *Nikawa,* shimmied her, bounced her in the confusion of waters, a violence that fulfilled my long wish for such an assertion of force. The moment had come, and my excitement to see our ascent begin quite purged my glooms. Facing the river that more than any other would decide whether or not we would make it to the Pacific gave me so much adrenaline and exuberance, quickened further by apprehension, I felt almost as if we were starting afresh. Herman Melville wrote, "He who has never been afar, let him once go from home to know what home is. For as you draw nigh again to your old native river, he seems to pour through you with all his tides, and in your enthusiasm you swear to build altars like milestones along both his sacred banks."

I'd waited for this moment not just since Elizabeth, New Jersey, but since I was ten or eleven years old when I wanted to know what it felt like in a small boat to enter the maw of the Missouri, the ruction of rivers, and I was glad for the high waters because I wanted it to deny us nothing. At last the river I grew up near, the one whose water I drank from birth until I went off to the Navy. The Big Muddy was in me, the source of my first blood, the humour in my bones, my definition of a river, a winding trickery that once nearly took me down, a flowing whose farthest stream is Hell Roaring Creek and which leaves the mountains under the shadow of a peak named Nemesis. We were about to go against it all the way to the mountains, to that place nine thousand feet above the sea where we could stand astride it and drink straight its native purity. . .

Befitting its nature, the Missouri comes snaking into the Mississippi on a bend five miles long before straightening perfectly into a reach that leads to another set of big bends. To hold in place this particular configuration at the confluence and to create a stable navigable channel, engineers have built along the first four miles thirty-five rock wing-dikes, structures that usually force even small boats to keep to the winding channel, but the stones were now well below the surface, and we were free to go nearly anywhere we saw wetness. The Piper took a position on the bow and played "Mist," "My Home," and, to make sure I was truly stirred to the challenge, another round of "Garry Owen," the Irish quickstep Indians like to whistle, the one that led George Custer's Seventh Cavalry into the tombs of history.

The Missouri is one of the fastest navigable rivers of length in the world, but as historian Stanley Vestal wrote, "The trouble with going up the Missouri River in a boat is that you have to take the boat along." For years a certain popular recreational cruising guide dismissed the river with the curt warning that it was "very hazardous to all boaters," but in the year of our ascent, the book at last included it, toning down the direful to a mere grousing "navigation [on the Missouri] is more a game of chance than a skilled profession." Reading that caution a day earlier, Pilotis had said, "Sounds like a perfect match for your brand of skippering."

The Piper had just come off the bow when *Nikawa* dropped into a virtual hole with a banging that shook our jawbones. It wasn't a true whirlpool but a large and ferocious eddy turning water, something a little less common than the numerous boils pushing currents upward, a less unnerving direction. I knew then, whatever else the Missouri did, it was not ever going to disappoint us; we could expect it, like a cross-grained grandfather, to do anything but bore us. We had the wind on our nose but only enough to ripple the water and leave the jouncings to the erratics of currents. And that's the way we started up the Missouri.

RIVERTOPS

TED WILLIAMS

Ted Williams is an editor-at-large and columnist for *Audubon* magazine, conservation editor of *Gray's Sporting Journal,* and a regular contributor to many environmental and outdoor publications, including *Mother Jones, National Wildlife,* and *Sierra.* He has had, as he says, "thirty-four years of environmental muckraking." He published his first article in *Audubon*—"Two Days Under Lake Dickey," about canoeing Maine's St. John River shortly before the U.S. Army Corps of Engineers dammed it in 1980. In 2001 he reported on the restoration of twenty-two miles of Florida's Kissimmee River, which had been straightened by the USACE in 1971 and renamed C-38—a restoration that came about largely because of public responses to articles he wrote. This essay, first published in *On Nature* (1986), is a celebration of his favorite river—a small trout stream in Massachusetts—and a lament for the passing of such vital threads of wilderness in an age that has seen "the irruption of my species."

. . .

HAVING ONE'S RIVERS is important, like having family or a country. With rivers, though, you get to choose. I prefer mine rippling with wild brook trout, which is to say clean and secluded, and because my time and place coincide with an irruption of my species, this means my rivers also must be small. Headwater streams really, the tops of systems known even in Boston's Back Bay.

An hour west of Worcester, Massachusetts, is the rivertop I love best. Hyla Brook, I call it, for that is not its name. Here under bald eagles and turkey vultures, in woods demanding good boots, lunch, the better part of a day and, sometimes, a compass, it's hard to remember you're not in Maine. In the general watershed are dozens of other brooks, some bigger than Hyla, some smaller, none quite so lovely. All are as safe from human defilement as is possible for running water to be, not because people enjoy their beauty or revel in the rich communities of plants and animals that flourish in and around them or spend time near them or in any way treasure them for what they are. Only because Boston drinks them.

Maybe Hyla Brook is someone else's, too, but of the hundreds of other anglers I have met along it over the years, not one has been human. My fellow killer apes are all miles downcurrent on the main stem, pretty enough in its own right, but stripped of wildness. There are dams and hardtop roads and metal bridges. And huge, sallow hatchery rainbow and brown trout, mutilated by months or years of scraping against the sides of concrete raceways. Sometimes their snouts are raw. Usually scales are missing, tails rounded and at least one pectoral fin gone or reduced to a fleshy stump. Almost without exception dorsals are matted and withered. A few of these fish even bear tags which may be exchanged for prizes. Last I knew they said "Make it in Mass."

From the high, lonesome ground of Hyla Brook, amid the trout lilies and trilliums, it is easy to wax pious, and I do not mean to criticize the state. Of all things it is called upon by the public to provide, it provides hatchery trout most efficiently. Massachusetts' hatchery system, in fact, is a clean, automated, computerized marvel that ought to be studied by every welfare department in the country.

It is the public demand rather than state compliance with it that needs scrutiny. Whatever is one to make of a culture that sets such a premium on sheer bigness? At least Dolly Parton sings well, but these alien, disfigured, inbred fish from Europe and the American West have only their size going for them, and even this is grotesque and unnatural in New England's usually sterile water.

How is it that we can spend such vast quantities of time and money distributing and collecting trout that don't belong while ignoring trout that do—our infinitely more beautiful land-locked char, *Salvelinus fontinalis,* the dweller of springs, the brook trout? It is not so in Europe where native browns are jealously conserved and natural recruitment demanded by those who angle for them.

Here we play "put and take" with imitation trout that couldn't reproduce in most Eastern water even if spawning habitat hadn't been flooded, silted or gouged and even if fish culturists hadn't thrown stock out of synch with the seasons in order to obtain "earlier eggs" and even if the planted fish (bred to be everything trout aren't, to thrive on trout kibbles amidst the quick-moving shadows of men and machines in coverless, concrete troughs) could commonly survive in the real world for more than several weeks. It is a game which renders natural spawning habitat superfluous.

And so we let our trout streams go to ruin except at their remote tops where ravishment is not yet convenient or where we have seen fit to protect our last undefiled watersheds like winos cradling the contents of their paper bags. As a child I caught hatchery trout in the Aberjona River, the ditched conduit that drains the world-famous toxic dumps of Woburn, Massachusetts. No need for American anglers to agitate for clean water; state government will provide fish even if nature can't. I suppose there is no sense sermonizing because we are no likelier to change our ways than the sea gulls who wheel and scream around fish-processing plants.

BETTER TO TELL what rivertop trouting is like, to encourage it, if not actually on Hyla Brook, at least on other forgotten Eastern rivertops that you can find yourself. I used to think that more native-brook-trout fishermen would mean fewer native brook trout. Now I think that the reverse is true, that more native-brook-trout fishermen mean more wild water preserved.

I first saw Hyla on a green topo map while ensconced in my easy chair beside a black-cherry fire. Having established that the brook was not on the state stocking list, a prerequisite for even casual consideration, I looked more closely at the map. Lots of unbroken green all around; I got interested. Gradient looked good; I got very interested. There were riffles and pools, and meadows where gaudy, stream-bred brook trout could sip mayflies and lounge in icy, air-charged current that tumbled down from hemlock-shaded ledges. I rushed there the next morning.

At this point I should note that finding healthy wild trout populations is like finding flying squirrels. You'll tap twenty or maybe a hundred hollow trees before a coal-eyed head appears. But troutlust is only one reason to find and keep rivertops. Rivertops are magnetized wires drawing and concentrating all the best things forests have. One may be equally infatuated with wildflowers or woodland butterflies or berries or woodpeckers or herons or deer or mink or beaver or drumming grouse or visions of silver spilling over moss . . . Come to think of it, to me each of these good things are all of them and more, and if I didn't hang around rivertops because of trout, it would be because of something else.

No day on a rivertop is ever better than your first. That magic morning on Hyla Brook ten Mays ago I had found one of the few spots in Massachusetts where you can hike hard for thirty minutes and be deeper into the woods than when you started—a secret, timeless place fragrant with skunk cabbage, leaf mulch and wet earth, where wood frogs quacked and redfin pickerel streaked from swampy shallows, where newts lay suspended in backwaters and sashayed into muck, where spring azures skipped among unfurling ferns and fields of watercress waved gently in clear current over clean gravel. In and out of the brook, clumps of marsh marigolds were in brilliant yellow bloom and, as far back as I could see, the banks were carpeted with pale yellow trout lilies. A pair of wood ducks burst from an ancient beaver flowage and went squealing downriver. Trout were too much to hope for.

Here and there, in the deeper pockets, I flipped out a puffy dry fly on a two-pound tippet, but nothing rose to it save fallfish—"chubs," trouters call them, spitting the word. Fallfish grunt like pigs. The bigger they are the louder they grunt. Once, in Maine, I ate one, and it tasted like wet Kleenex. But something about Hyla Brook made me look hard at fallfish, and I saw them for the first time not as "trash fish" to be squeezed and bush-tossed, but as a part that belonged. Really, they are quite beautiful, very streamlined, silver in their youth, bronze and pewter in maturity. Thoreau, who fished for them passionately, called them "chivin" and basically found them to be "cupreous dolphin."

Not expecting trout, I naturally found them, suddenly and in astonishing abundance. They were rising to little blue mayflies in the deep, quick water at the head of the first meadow exactly as I had imagined the night before. I pushed through thick alders, wiping spiderwebs from my face and grimacing as ice water rose to my waist. Finally, feeling like Sylvester tossed into the birdcage and told to help himself, I was in position. The fly drifted about six inches before it disappeared in a lusty boil. It is difficult for brook-trout anglers to admit, but the brutal truth

is that these noble fish not only are nonselective in their feeding behavior, but reckless, suicidal even. One can "match the
hatch" if one chooses or one can toss out a Japanese machine-
tied Bumble Boogie. Nine times out of ten the results will be the
same—instant slurp.

That first trout from Hyla Brook was the third biggest I
have ever taken there—eleven inches. (I won't say I set *no* premium on bigness.) She ran the line around a beaver cutting,
and I reached down and tickled her smooth flanks, lifting her
toward the surface so slowly she never struggled until she was
on the bank. She was perfectly proportioned, deep-bodied, with
a smallish head indicative of good feed and fast growth. The
markings on her green back resembled old worm trails on the
inside of elm bark, and her chestnut sides were flecked with scarlet, each fleck ringed with blue. Her belly was orange, pectoral,
ventral and anal fins crimson and trimmed with ivory. I fished on
for two miles, catching wild brook trout all the way—little fish
of big country—and at dusk a great horned owl floated out of the
woods and settled on a drowned cedar under a crescent moon.

There have been scores of other important days on Hyla
Brook: The time I got there late and couldn't tear myself away
and got lost in the drizzly dark, plowing till 2:00 AM through
grape and jewelweed with only the cold, green light of fireflies
all around, feeling like Bottom in *Midsummer Night's Dream*.
The time I almost stepped on a deer. The time last year I sat on a
sandbar, cleaning trout in the bright moonlight and listening to
Eastern coyotes howling and moving on the hill in back of me.

I want more people on rivertops, but it does not follow that I want more of them on mine. Rivertops are very personal things, like axes and shotguns, and I have shared mine only with a seven-year-old named Beth and a ten-year-old named Scott. Rivertops are not to be tattled on. To quote my friend John Voelker, the sage of Michigan's U.P. who quit the state's supreme court in order to chase brook trout and write about them and who, having made it well past eighty, has earned the right to be sexist, "Any fisherman who will tell on the trout waters that are revealed to him possesses the stature of a man who will tell on the women he's dallied with."

"[Wild] trout, unlike men," writes Voelker, "will not—indeed cannot—live except where beauty dwells, so that any man who would catch a trout finds himself inevitably surrounded by beauty: he can't help himself." That's what I've been trying to say.

KEVIN VAN TIGHEM

Kevin Van Tighem has worked most of his life as a biologist and inter-
preter in western Canada's national parks system. He has published
widely on wildlife and conservation issues, and his essays have been collected in two volumes, *Coming West: A Natural History of Home* (1997)
and *Home Range: Writings on Conservation and Restoration* (2000). "The
Tree and the Trout," reprinted here from the former, points to the intricate
and unsuspected connectedness of natural ecosystems and was originally
written as a protest against the damming of Alberta's Oldman River. Van
Tighem lives in Waskesiu, Saskatchewan, where he is superintendent of
Prince Albert National Park.

. . .

EACH FALL, WHEN cottonwood leaves turn yellow and begin
to set sail on the October breezes, brown trout come up the
Bow. Some turn and ascend the Elbow River to spawn below
Glenmore Dam. Others remain in the Bow, forging upstream

through Calgary, Alberta, to spawning beds in the backwaters and riffles below the Bearspaw Dam.

By the time the first ice begins to form around streamside boulders, another spawning season is over. The trout retreat to their wintering holes to wait out another long winter.

Seasons come and go along the river; the trout spawn and return; the years roll by.

Although I grew up only three blocks from the Bow, it was not until I was in high school that I first fished the big river. It was a challenge for a boy who had grown up fishing small headwater creeks. Nonetheless, I soon learned how to catch the abundant little rainbow trout in the long riffles upstream from the Crowchild Bridge.

I was an aspiring fly tier with a nervous dog. His tail developed a zigzag, patchy look during my Bow River phase. Each time he saw me coming with the scissors he would cringe and try to tuck his tattered tail beneath his belly. I tied flies that I called "bucktails," for lack of a better term. "Dogtail" was not in any of the books I had read. It was a simple pattern: little bits of Tim's tail tied onto a hook wrapped with Christmas tree tinsel. I anchored the whole thing down with Mom's sewing thread and my brother's model airplane glue. It worked just as well as the more expensive creations I could not afford and lacked the skill to tie.

Each evening after supper, I grabbed my fly rod and headed down to fish the river till dark. Throughout September, I usually managed to catch the odd little rainbow. By mid-October, however, when streamside foliage was golden and the river full of floating, soggy leaves, the rainbows no longer fed so eagerly in the evenings. Drifting leaves, like submerged booby traps, confounded my fishing as the streetlights flickered to life across the river. I sometimes fished several minutes before realizing I was casting a piece of sodden vegetation. Rafts of brown and yellow foliage eventually blanketed the eddy at the toe of my favourite run, making it virtually impossible to fish.

One evening I let my homemade fly drift into the accumulation of leaf litter. There was a bulging of the river's surface, so subtle in the near-dark and streetlight-flicker that I almost missed it. I set the hook instinctively, and was suddenly fast to a big trout.

The fish pulled me helplessly after him as he ran, sulked, ran and held again, working steadily downstream toward the dark outline of the Crowchild Bridge. At length I wrestled him ashore. I raced home to show the biggest fish I had caught until then—an eighteen-inch brown trout—to Mom and Dad.

When I think back on my finest brown trout fishing trips, the picture that comes to mind always seems to have poplars in it. Golden cottonwoods lining the Bow River late in the fall; balsam poplars turning silver in the wind as a June thunderstorm rolls across the Fallentimber; the glistening, summer-green foliage of black cottonwoods crowding the lower Crowsnest.

The biggest browns hide beneath logjams formed by old cottonwoods, washed out by spring floods. What do you snag your backcast in? Poplars. Where do the salmon flies and golden stones take refuge in the short weeks between the crazy fishing of the stonefly hatch and the equally crazy fishing of the egg-laying flight? The poplar canopy.

Anglers fish all day surrounded by wind-chatter in poplar foliage, then lean against the grooved bark of an old cottonwood for lunch. The vireos and orioles that serenade June mornings—background music for countless great fishing trips—nest in the cottonwood canopy. In the grassy, windblown outer foothills, eager anglers watch for ribbons of green showing where their favourite trout streams burrow through sheltering galleries of poplar forest—black cottonwood, Plains cottonwood, nar-rowleaf cottonwood, balsam poplar.

It is more than mere coincidence that cottonwoods and brown trout live together in the landscape, and in our minds.

Cheryl Bradley studies forest ecology in southern Alberta. Several years ago she became curious about why cottonwoods were growing scarcer along many rivers both in Canada and the USA.

Cheryl mapped the native range of the plains cottonwood, the largest and most spectacular of the poplar family. All along the western edge of its range the cottonwood lines some of the most famous trout streams in North America: the Missouri, Big Hole, Beaverhead, Yellowstone, Platte, Bighorn and others.

Those are potent names in the minds of most serious trout anglers. As a teenager, I used to buy back-issues of the big three American sporting magazines at a used-book store in Hillhurst. After covetously poring over accounts of great Montana and

Wyoming trout rivers, I would go down to the Bow and fish beneath the cottonwoods. I had no way of knowing at the time that the only difference between my rivers and theirs was that nobody had written mine up yet.

Like the famous American rivers, the Bow is full of big browns and rainbows. Like those other rivers, cottonwoods line its banks. And like most of those other rivers, Cheryl learned, the cottonwood stands are gradually dying out and failing to replenish themselves.

Recently, several anglers who regularly fish the lower Bow River began calling for action to protect the river's cottonwoods from beavers. At several points along the river below Calgary, the rodents continue to fell the big trees. There are few young poplars to replace them. Some anglers wrap chicken wire around the bases of trees near the water's edge to deter the beavers.

The problem, however, is not beavers. And, as Cheryl Bradley's graduate research revealed, there may be little we can do to save those beautiful floodplain forests.

The Milk River—where Cheryl did her earliest research—supports at least as many beavers, and far more cottonwoods, than the lower Bow. Most springs bring a new crop of cottonwoods to replace those lost to beavers or washed out by spring flooding. Along the Bow, however, springtime usually brings few washed out trees and fewer cottonwood seedlings.

Cheryl found that the life of the river and the life of the cottonwood are intimately connected. Disrupt one, and you disrupt the other.

The big streams that drain east from the Rockies into North America's Great Plains are volatile creatures. They flood each spring when the mountain snowpack melts and spring rains peak. By late May or early June, they are brown and ugly with runoff. Overflowing their banks, they spill into side channels and swales. Where water overflows or slows, silt settles out, enriching floodplain soils.

Along the main channel, the swollen river erodes the upstream sides of meander bends where the current is most powerful. The river balances its destructive work by depositing silt, sand and washed-out trees on the sheltered downstream sides of the bends, where the current is most gentle. Rivers like the Milk can rework their entire floodplains every decade or two.

Later in the summer, river flow drops to only a fraction of what it was during the spring flow. Through late summer and fall, the river depends on headwater forests that act as sponges, trapping rainfall and releasing it slowly into springs and creeks that sustain the shrunken river.

Cottonwoods set seed in June, when the spring runoff is at its peak. Billions of white, fluffy seeds set sail on the wind, drifting along the valleys until they find something damp to stick to. Many seeds eventually lodge at the edge of the flooding river on newly deposited point bars. There they sprout in a silty, well-watered seedbed.

Natural rivers follow much the same seasonal pattern of flood and ebb from year to year. The following June, consequently, usually brings a new layer of silt to bury the seedlings a little deeper. The flood waters also irrigate the young trees just when they need it most. If the river does not let them down for the first two or three years of life, the fast-growing young cottonwoods have no problem surviving.

Since the river reworks its floodplain annually, meanders migrate slowly down-valley over the passing years, as upstream edges wash out and downstream edges build up. The cottonwood forest migrates with the river. The youngest trees are always on the downstream sides of the bends, and the oldest on the upstream sides, where spring floods eventually washed them out.

Cottonwoods are becoming sparser along so many rivers from Alberta south to Texas because government water engineers have dammed most western rivers to regulate their flows.

A few foothills rivers, like the Highwood and the Belly, merely have diversion weirs that tilt some of the river's water into side valleys. However, large onstream dams plug the Red Deer, Bow, St. Mary's, Waterton and most other western rivers.

When water slows, it loses its ability to carry sand and silt. That is why rivers form deltas where they enter lakes and oceans. That is also why the reservoirs that form behind dams become giant silt traps during the muddy floods of springtime.

Cheryl Bradley and other researchers have found that downstream from dams, rivers cut down into the meanders they occupied before the dam's construction. Without the silt that it has lost to the bottom of the reservoir behind the dam, the river mines its own bed to restore its equilibrium. The meanders stop migrating and become entrenched. Cottonwood seeds, consequently, can no longer sprout on new point bars.

The water engineers who operate the dams use them to store spring flood waters. Again, this works against any young cottonwoods that manage to sprout downstream from the dam. Thirsty young seedlings can no longer rely on the spring floods as reliable sources of irrigation water.

New cottonwoods sprout too infrequently along the dammed, regulated rivers to keep pace with the death of the old trees.

That is what is happening along the Bow River today. Dr. Stewart Rood, a professor at the University of Lethbridge, has found a similar thing happening on the St. Mary's—which has lost more than half its cottonwoods since engineers dammed it in 1952—and the Waterton River, which has lost a quarter of its cottonwoods since they dammed it in the 1960s.

The same thing will happen when Alberta Environment's water engineers finish building the notorious Oldman River Dam. This goes a long way in explaining the determination with which many Peigan Indians—whose reserve is downstream from the dam and to whom the cottonwood forests are sacred—continue their legal battle to have the dam shut down.

For anglers, however, maybe dams are not all bad. Admittedly, the eventual loss of cottonwoods might make the valley a little less scenic and a bit less pleasant on a hot summer's day. Perhaps those are small prices to pay, however, considering that dammed rivers control flows of water all year round. After all, the Bow River's Bearspaw Dam controls flows in the lower Bow.

That flow control has played a big role in creating the internationally acclaimed lower Bow River fishery.

However, the cottonwood, the river and the trout are linked in more ways than one.

When cottonwoods turn golden and begin to shed their leaves in October, foothills and prairie rivers are at low ebb. Riffles are shallow and weak, backwaters flaccid; the rivers are sleepy.

Those same winds that spread cottonwood seeds in June still funnel down the valleys. Now, however, they pick up the golden wealth of thousands of big trees and whip the carbohydrate-rich leaves back and forth along the floodplain. Millions of dead leaves alight in the river, grow sodden, and sink.

Underwater, bacteria and fungus set to work decomposing the leaves. Beetle and caddis larvae munch away at the soggy harvest. Mayfly and stonefly nymphs feed on the smaller bits and the excretions of other invertebrates. Midge and blackfly larvae and net-spinning caddis filter bits of leaf debris out of the current. Willowfly and dragonfly nymphs hunt the river bed, preying on the leaf-eaters.

Whole guilds of insects rely on the leaf litter, processing and re-processing it as the seasons turn. Salmonflies grow large and protein-rich on organic detritus throughout the summer, fall and winter. When spring floods arrive to scour away the worked-over leaf litter, the salmonfly nymphs crawl ashore, hatch, and fly up . . . to shelter in the new year's crop of poplar leaves.

The river sustains the trees. The trees sustain the insect life. And the insect life sustains the trout.

Downstream from Calgary, the Bow River fishery will probably survive the depletion of that river's cottonwoods. The Bow has a substitute for poplar leaves; an entire city fertilizes the river with treated sewage.

But the lonely trout streams that drain the high plains—Willow Creek, the Oldman, Waterton and St. Mary's—have no such easy substitute. Their chief source of organic enrichment is their riparian mosaics of poplars, willows and other shrubbery. Those living mosaics rely on the natural rhythms of spring freshet and autumn drought to sustain them. And Alberta's water engineers have built lucrative careers out of rearranging those natural rhythms.

In the case of the Oldman River, the Alberta government has enlisted Stewart Rood to help them develop an operating plan for their new dam. They are counting on the plant ecologist's advice to help them save, or at least slow the loss of, the spectacular cottonwood forests all the way downstream to Lethbridge. Rood hopes that the dam operators can sustain cottonwoods by releasing water in a way that mimics the spring flood, and by keeping the floodplain well-supplied with water all summer.

Cheryl Bradley is less optimistic. She points out that there is no way of restoring the silt and sediments trapped in the upstream reservoir. Without that sediment, the mock spring floods are more likely to scour out the river bed than to enrich the floodplain. Looking at the rivers that drain the high plains and foothills of the American West, where many dams have been in place for decades, ecologists see little cause for optimism. Most streams have lost, or are losing, much of their riparian forest.

Whatever the fate of the Oldman's floodplain forests, the controversy over the dam that threatens them offers a useful lesson. If we are to sustain the fisheries we have inherited, more by luck than by good planning, anglers must look beyond the trout and water engineers must look beyond the water. Those who wish to assert an unearned right to rearrange rivers would be wise to first learn to see the whole ecosystem in all its complexity—the subtle, intricate and inescapable connections among winds, and seasons, and floods, and trees, and soils, and leaves, and trout, and human decisions. It might temper their ambitions.

Certainly the seventeen-year-old angler fishing the darkened Bow River, while balsam poplars whispered in the wind and leaves floated past in the surface film, had no idea that those trees were anything more than scenery. He had no way of seeing that their leaves were anything other than a nuisance. He never suspected that those trees were not only part of his fishing experience, but, ultimately, part of his river, and part of his fish.

He understands a little more now. And that understanding has raised a new and troubling question. To what extent will those trees be part of his future?

ADORATION OF
A HOSE

DAVID JAMES DUNCAN

A native of Portland, Oregon, David James Duncan published his first
novel, *The River Why*, in 1980. His first nonfiction book, *River Teeth*,
appeared in 1991 and was written from "a sense of betrayal, out of rage over
natural systems violated, out of grief for a loved world raped, and out of a
craving for justice." Like Kevin Van Tighem and Ted Williams, Duncan
avidly supports wilderness preservation and is an outspoken critic of clear-
cutting and river-damming projects. He won the 2001 Western States Book
Award for *My Story as Told by Water,* from which this excerpt is taken, and
in 2003 received the American Library Association's Eli Oboler Award
for the Preservation of Intellectual Freedom for *Citizen's Dissent,* which
he co-authored with nature writer and poet Wendell Berry. In the following excerpt, Duncan recounts his earliest encounters with flowing water,
experiences that triggered a lifelong obsession with rivers. He lives in
Lolo, Montana.

. . .

I WAS BORN in a hospital located on the flanks of a volcanic cone. This cone, named Mount Taber, looks as innocent as an overturned teacup as it rises over a densely populated section of Southeast Portland, Oregon. Decades before my birth, scientists had of course declared the cone to be unimpeachably extinct. The hospital, however, afforded a nice view of another cone, thirty-five miles away in the same volcanic system, also declared extinct in those days: Mount St. Helens. Forgive my suspicion of certain unimpeachable declarations of science.

My birth-cone's slopes were drained by tiny seasonal streams, which, like most of the creeks in that industrialized quadrant of Portland, were buried in underground pipes long before I arrived on the scene. There were also three small reservoirs on Mount Taber's slopes, containing the water that bathed me at birth, water I would drink for eighteen years, water that gave me life. But this water didn't come from Mount Taber, or from the surrounding hills, or even from the aquifer beneath: it came, via concrete and iron flumes, from the Bull Run River, which drains the slopes of the Cascade Mountains forty miles away.

I was born, then, without a watershed. On a planet held together by gravity and fed by rain, a planet whose every creature depends on water and whose every slope works full-time, for eternity, to create creeks and rivers, I was born with neither. The creeks of my birth-cone were invisible, the river from somewhere else entirely. Of course millions of Americans are now born this way. And many of them grow up without creeks, live lives lacking intimacy with rivers, and become well-adjusted, productive citizens even so.

Not me. The dehydrated suburbs of my boyhood felt as alien to me as Mars. The arid industrial life into which I was being prodded looked to me like the life of a Martian. What *is* a Martian? Does Mars support intelligent life? I had no idea. My early impression of the burgeoning burbs and urbs around me was of internally-combusting hordes of dehydrated beings manufacturing and moving unnecessary objects from one place to another in order to finance the rapid manufacture and transport of more unnecessary objects. Running water, on the other hand, felt as necessary to me as food, sleep, parents, and air. And on the cone of my birth, all such water had been eliminated.

I didn't rebel against the situation. Little kids don't rebel. That comes later, along with the hormones. What I did was hand-build my own rivers—breaking all neighborhood records, in the process, for amount of time spent running a garden hose. In the beginning, in Southeast Portland, there was nothing much there at all. Dehydrated Martians seemed to cover the place completely. So I would fasten the family hose to an azalea bush at the uphill end of one of my mother's sloping flower beds, turn the faucet on as hard as Mom would allow, and watch hijacked Bull Run River water spring forth in an arc and start cutting a minuscule, audible river (*ka*) down through the bed. I'd then camp by this river all day.

As my river ran and ran, the thing my mother understandably hated and I understandably loved began to happen: *creation*.

The flower-bed topsoil slowly washed away, and a streambed of tiny colored pebbles gradually appeared: a bed that soon looked just like that of a genuine river, complete with tiny point bars and cutbanks, meanders and eddies, fishy-looking riffles, slow pools. It was a nativity scene, really: the entire physics and fluvial genius of Gravity-Meets-Water-Meets-Earth incarnating in perfect miniature. I built matchbook-sized hazelnut rafts and cigarette-butt-sized elderberry canoes, launched them on my river, let them ride down to the gargantuan driveway puddle that served as my Pacific. I stole a three-inch-tall blue plastic cavalry soldier from my brother's Fort Apache set, cut the stock off his upraised rifle so that only the long, flexible barrel remained, tied a little thread to the end of the barrel to serve as fly line, and set the soldier fishing. I'd then lie flat on my belly, cheek to the ground, and stare at this U.S. Cavalry dropout, thigh-deep in his tiny river, rifle-rod high in the air, line working in the current; stare till I became him; stare till, in the sunlit riffle, we actually hooked and landed tiny sun-glint fish. "Shut off that hose!" my mother would eventually shout out the kitchen window. "You've turned the whole driveway into a mudhole!"

Poor woman, I'd think. *It's not a mudhole. It's a tide flat.*

I'd gladly turn the hose off, though: that's how I got the tide to go out. I'd then march my river soldier out onto the flat, to dig for clams.

BANK DEPOSITS

TREVOR HERRIOT

A naturalist, writer, and illustrator, Trevor Herriot has lived most of his life in Saskatchewan. He has published two books, *Jacob's Wound: A Search for the Spirit of Wilderness* (2004) and *River in a Dry Land: A Prairie Passage* (2000), which won the Drainie-Taylor Biography Prize as well as the Regina Book Award, and from which this account of growing up on the Qu'Appelle River, east of Regina, Saskatchewan, near the Manitoba border, is taken. Herriot explores the prairie landscape and our relationship to the land with gentle insight, reminding us that rivers are useful as well as spiritual and majestic. He lives in Regina, where he hosts a CBC Radio program for birders called *Birdline*.

. . .

ON THE AFTERNOON I took my mother and Aunt Doris out to walk over the old yard site at the mouth of the Little Cutarm, I thought of the derelict house I saw there as a child: siding stripped grey by the years, doors open, windows gone, the smell of damp flooring and mouse urine, and the holes in the walls where the McRae girls, craving calcium or some other mineral, would tear off chunks of plaster to gnaw upon. The building was salvaged for lumber twenty-some years ago, and it has probably been at least that long since these two urban McRae sisters walked the place together and allowed its ghosts to recall their origins.

As we walked, one memory arose, settled and faded into the next, spanning the years of their life in the house my grandfather built in 1921: the house they were born in seventy years ago; the house they left as teenagers some fifty years ago; the house that was empty soon after and that became in my time a wind-worn monument to the floor-sweeping, pail-slopping existence that was once here, until it vanished leaving nothing but stories behind. Stories that weather the memory as peak moments capped and hardened by humour, grief, or drama—odd figures crystallized within the soft, eroding drift of days and left standing like hoodoos in the heart's terrain.

There is the story I call The Soul's Awakening. This was the title of an illustration that hung on the living-room wall of the McRae home, where the girls admired it every day of their childhood. It was one of those inspirational religious paintings still found in the church basements of this region: a radiant young woman, eyes turned upward to a glow from beyond the picture—is it heaven or a vision of the Lord?—her hair and face as dazzling as any Hollywood star's of the 1920s, but different, for her countenance is flooded with innocence and wonder at the cause of her awakening. And Margaret looked just like her when she came home for visits from the city—Margaret Tinnics, Lewis's big sister, the neighbour's girl who had moved to Regina to work for Government Telephones and who came home sometimes on Saturdays with gifts for everyone, hats and coats for her parents and siblings, and a huge steamer trunk full of clothes she had grown tired of and donated to the girls back in West Valley; and who had fancy combs and brushes and fashion jewellery; and who told of the modern conveniences that made life richer, easier, and more exciting in the city; and who had changed her name to Marguerite Tinnish because it looked and sounded better and you could do that in the city; and who was glamorous and sophisticated and generous and rich. When the McRae girls knew Margaret was coming for a weekend they would sit and wait for her high on one of the hills so they could see a long way down the valley and watch the road for any sign of her, and as they waited they imagined themselves one day taking the same road to a life where instead of jumper stew and baring your arse to the breeze, there would be market food and porcelain toilets, a life worth coming home from, like Margaret, bearing trinkets and the glow of a soul's awakening.

I WALKED OVER to the edge of the foundation while my mother eased her way into the bottom of the cellar depression. Aunt Doris picked up something oval-shaped and nickel-plated.

"It's from the front of the old stove." She paused, looking up from the artifact to her sister rummaging in the cellar.

"Remember how the oven door was broken and mother had a stick of oak jammed between it and the floor to keep it closed, and we'd always run through the kitchen and trip on it?"

We looked for places, patches of ground they remembered: for the flat rock on which Snooks swears he fried an egg one scorching day in July and for the maples growing rank like weeds in the rich soil of the squatting place the McRaes called, with a nod to gentility, "the ash pile," and for the place where Jock would stand in the yard to direct his voice up toward Bruce's Point, where his daughter-in-law Bea would be standing a half-mile away on the edge of the hill to take his order—and here Aunt Doris faced the point, pressed her chin down to lower her voice, and offered her best rendition, with r's rolling and t's slurred, of the old man shouting, "Bring me some buttermilk!"

Something brought the Lebanese peddlers to mind: Sam and Leo Joseph, swarthy exotic-smelling fellows, coming down the valley road with two dray horses pulling a van full of brushes, linen, spices, and an assortment of products—everything from egg-beaters to gopher poison—for easing the housewife's burden. Millie would always feed them and then invite them to stay the night before they passed on up the Qu'Appelle along their circuit. And then there were the railcar hobos, jumping off the train as the CPR made the turn from the valley into the Little Cutarm at the edge of their fields. Like the itinerant peddlers, they knew the yard, had it marked: "kind lady, bread." One tramp used to come regularly for a slab of bread dipped in bacon grease—a treat he could rely on from the farm where the line turned north at the first creek west of Tantallon.

My mother wanted to walk down to a certain bend in the river where they would go to wash clothes in the summertime. The washing place, she said, was just west of the confluence of the creek and the river, where a stretch of sand formed the instep of a bend. We made our way down to the river, following a trail across a cultivated field that had been colonized by bluegrass, crested wheat grass, and alfalfa. I was surprised to find a good-sized patch of big bluestem, the eastern Qu'Appelle's showy native tallgrass, that appears to have reclaimed a corner of the field. The trail petered out into a maze of game pathways entering the willows alongside oxbow ponds. These stagnant ponds found everywhere along the length of the valley are the scars of the Calling River's recent history—crescent-shaped chunks of river that were cut off from the active channel when it formed a shortcut between the nearest points of a meander.

A bend in a prairie river like the Qu'Appelle can wander a long way in fifty years. As we crashed in and out of the bush, it occurred to me that the old washing place is more than likely a silted-in oxbow pond by now. There was no point in explaining meander mechanics to my mother, so I searched through the riverside willows until I found what is now the first bend west of the confluence. And then she told me again, as she had dozens of times before, how the McRaes washed their clothes.

"In the summertime, on a warm day, Mother would hitch up a horse to the stone boat and take us girls down here to the river for the afternoon. On the stone boat the horse pulled two barrels: one empty and the other loaded with dirty clothes. We'd play in the shallows at the riverside while Mother piled up stones and built a fire under a barrel of water. The water'd get hot, and she'd start scrubbing the clothes on her washboard. We helped her hang the clean things on the willows to dry. By then we'd all be hot, so Mother, red in the face from the heat and the work, would come into the river with us and we'd all swim and splash around. Later, when it was time to head back to the house, we'd put the clean clothes in one barrel and fill the other one with river water to use in the kitchen. Every two weeks or so we'd do that."

In 1858, James Austin Dickinson, the surveyor-naturalist on the Hind expedition through the Qu'Appelle country, came across a group of Saulteaux women downstream from Crooked Lake as he paddled his way along the eastern half of the river. The women were washing and playing in the river. The life of these women, who scurried, laughing, to retrieve their clothes on shore, was alien and inscrutable to Dickinson, good servant of God and Queen. It is Dickinson I think of when I consider all that separates me from the riverside lives of the women in my mother's washday reminiscence.

My family's laundry is handled by Karen and a box that comes from Sears—an electrified, engineered box that churns soap packaged in Toronto with water filtered, chlorinated, and piped forty-five miles from Buffalo Pound Lake to our urban basement. Convenient, little scrubbing required, but no nickering horse, no soughing willows, no sandy shallows in which to splash with the children.

Wascana Creek, old Pile o' Bones, runs through Regina a half-mile south of our house, but washing clothes there would be futile—an exchange of one kind of filth for another and possibly a violation of civic bylaws. Doing laundry once every two weeks at the river, though it was undoubtedly less pleasant than it appears beneath the gloss of memory, was one of the lighter tasks within the unending cycle of chores that passed through the hands of my grandmother and other women of her class and time. Indoor plumbing has eased many of these tasks, and we have to a great degree formed our culture by changing the way our mothers, wives, and daughters feed and clothe the members of their households. The costs, in terms of community and ecology, however, have been high.

When we stepped away from the riverside and began piping water into our homes, out of taps and down sewers, we lost touch with what may be the only sound way of living on the prairie—in respectful proximity with the gathering of scarce water. I will sometimes sit on the rim of the valley above the Big Cutarm, or the south end of Lake Katepwe, or other places where the Métis settled in the Qu'Appelle and I will try to envision the land sectioned in long lots running back from the river, up the round hills to the prairie above. Given a different history, a different outcome at Batoche and Duck Lake, the Métis system of land allotment might have kept us nearer the waterways and valleys that have sustained prairie people for thousands of years. Living out of sight of the river has put it out of mind, allowing us to forget that beyond the artificial and tenuous support of petrochemicals and an economy dependent on distant trade, water—its quantity and quality—is still the great arbiter of life in a semi-arid climate, the genius that shapes the character of our households, our communities, and our poetry as a grassland people.

As we walked back from the washing place it occurred to me that we might all be better off if we spent more time at river banks and less at the other kind. What if we gave our river-banks credit for all that we borrow from them? What if we made careful withdrawals and deposits worthy of the river? What if we made up for our debts there? If we calculated the interest charged by a river, the price of our endless borrowing, the possibility of foreclosure? And if recovering from "bank failure" involved building a fence to keep the cattle out of the willows?

SUPERIOR

JILL FRAYNE

Jill Frayne grew up in Toronto, one of four children of writers June Call-wood and Trent Frayne. She began her relationship with nature after moving to the nearby rural community of Uxbridge. When a long-term relationship ended and her daughter left home to go to university, she decided to take a three-month trip to the Yukon and northern British Columbia. The journey was recounted in her first book, *Starting Out in the Afternoon: A Mid-Life Journey into Wild Land* (2002), in which the depth and solace of her connection to new landscapes continually astonished her. Along the way she took up sea kayaking, and it is from a chapter on kayaking on Lake Superior, with its evocation of the haunting vastness and perils associated with that Great Lake, that this passage is taken.

. . .

TERRACE BAY IS A PULP and paper town on the north shore, the shortest point between the mainland and the Slate Islands. When we got there it began to rain and the wind cut off, the lake still rolling and huffing but setting up no whitecaps. The islands were suddenly very close. We went down to the beach to look. It was drizzling and glum, but there was a channel of smooth water past the surf zone, safe access onto the lake. We had a chance.

I knew I'd be the one to say the word, and I said, "Well, let's go." The men whooped and we went into motion like things that have been drifting at random and suddenly coalesce and find their purpose. This crossing is what we came to do. We took the boats off the roofs and down to the shore, pried the hatch covers off, wadded bundle after bundle below decks. We moved the cars away and locked up, took to the bushes to worm into our wetsuits and clammy paraphernalia, traded off final impossible items to whoever had a pocket of room. Jack took my frying pan and billy, strapped the covers on his hatches, rammed his hat on his head and eased the tail of his boat into the water. I was already floating, my hands trembling on my paddle. We made our way out past the surf zone and the bottom fell away.

The lake was in a state of queasy, lolling swells; some monstrous thing, temporarily dozing off. I put my rudder down, yanked my hat and gloves off, got Jack on my right side, thirty feet away. I would have liked to tie myself to him, but it wouldn't have helped. I couldn't rest, not trusting the slack, wanting to drag the islands closer. I paddled the twelve kilometres without a break, Jack rising and falling serenely beside me on ten-foot swells, Graham and Adrienne on our other side, keeping company. After a while I was warding off seasickness and needed to keep my paddle in the water to brace and ground.

The wind held off. We got into a gap between the islands and the big waves stopped. We paddled into a bay in late sun, and it was like coming into a Haida camp a hundred years ago, the water crystal and still, the steep beach sickle-shaped, caked in rolling pebbles, the trees backlit, laying shade into the water.

We landed, and jumped for joy. We'd left the world and come here on our own power, and we were all alone. Even the birds had gone.

It does remind me of Haida Gwaii—the pure water, cobble beaches, collapsing wild woods. Here, it's spruce trees, thin and toppling, wrapped in crinkled green lichen. The ground is thick with autumn rot and windfall, a million shooting spores, wet-scented fungus and mushrooms, caribou trails.

We hiked today, explored the body of our island, taking the caribou labyrinth in an arc that brought us down again to the shore, following a maze of trails the animals have made, elegant and steady, the easiest, most logical route over the island. The forest is hectic and magical, the spruce trees pressing on one another, the individual trees fragile, their lower branches thin and brittle, reaching straight out and frequently snapped off. Jack thinks they are being devoured by the lichen covering them. In a coastal way, the fallen ones nurse other growth, a wild rumple of mosses and lichens of every kind. There are thousands of mushrooms, frail ones with filament stalks and tiny, brilliant knobs, huge saffron umbrellas on top of milky stems. These plants are pure sex; minute, unabashed genitals, a slippery, showy fusion of male and female that's part thrusting and part rilled and round.

We follow a path that takes us up to the crest of the island, to a southern view of the near islands and out over an empty, aluminum surface as far as the eye can see. We go down again to the shore and walk back along peach-coloured slate that is turned on edge like a worn deck of cards, softened and smoothed where the waterline has worked it away.

After lunch the others go paddling and I walk down the beach. The hills rise steep, aspen-covered, the trees turning amber, dark spires of spruce shooting through the gold. Along the waterline the dark rock is splashed with orange lichen. Mountain ash are in berry along the shore. Paddling in yesterday to the camp that Jack remembered, we passed many beaches, always stone, some so fine and smooth we could drag the kayaks up on them, some pale and jagged, some cobble. Each of them has a huge throw of driftwood high above the waterline, the print of winter storms.

The wind is in the east the next morning, an opportunity to visit the rugged south side. We are tucked in our boats before the rain starts, a fine, out-of-the-way drizzle. We paddle round the west point, and after a while there is nothing to my right but horizon and on the left, huge beaches, a succession of ragged coves, sheer and tremendous, grottoes draped in ferns, mad sculptures shaped by waves, juts of rock set on edge straight as ships. Between two massive capes of rock, boulders the size of cars are jammed, flung there who knows when. Farther on, a wall of rock has shattered but holds intact, keeping its cracked form like a windshield in a wreck. We paddle from one fabulous view to the next, like tourists with the wonders of the world lined up for us. We land in an enormous curve of tiny pebbles and eat in thin rain on six feet of dry beach under a leaning shelf of rock. Graham hands out soup, and we are grinning. We feel like castaways. This is all we hoped for, the best it could be.

After lunch I do not want to go on to the lighthouse at the halfway point and decide to start back. I have a constant sense of pushing my luck in this extreme place. Jack accompanies me and we go slowly, trailing into the shallow coves we passed this morning. One has a floor like crusted jewels, rose and turquoise stone in crystal water, the dark walls cupping over our heads.

The rain strengthens and a headwind comes on. We paddle side by side, resting behind an island before the last leg. We see Graham and Adrienne coming along in their tandem, the only moving shapes in a dim grey ball of water and sky. . .

We meant to leave yesterday but put it off because of a fine south wind, perfect wind to paddle to the south side again and perfect wind, if it had held, to push us back to Terrace Bay. We don't know what the weather has in store: the radio batteries gave out.

In the event, the wind changed. We had our splendid day yesterday and glided down our island early this morning prepared to make the crossing. When we left the lee, the north wind broke on us so forcefully we could barely make headway. Paddling as hard as we could, we tacked east to another island and landed behind it. Nothing to do but wait out the wind.

The next day was the first day of October, the month of storms, and we get as far as the sandbar we landed on days ago, the two-sided beach Graham calls a tombola, bounded on one end by a high bloom of land, and joined at the other to the main part of the island. We have now moved to the farthest edge of shelter. There's nowhere to go but across Jackfish Channel to the mainland.

We wait differently. Adrienne and I are content. After a morning of slashing rain, the weather clears and we move around our narrow turf in bright wind, keeping a little fire going, making teas and soup, the two of us assenting to the temper of the lake. Graham paces, watches the wind rough the water, thinks how to get us out. Jack spans the difference, temperamentally more ready to wait than Graham but sympathetic to the task of getting home. The two stand bundled against the wind, conferring.

We are probably not in mortal danger. If we try the crossing, the waves, so far, are not big enough to capsize us, but we are at risk of wearing out against the wind and being forced far off course. We have no radio contact, no forecast, no chance of passersby, a limit to our food.

Jack and I take a walk in the afternoon along the trails to the south, with high views of the coast and spongy breaks in the trees, where we crouch and watch the wind tear at the water. Wind rocks the woods, the little spruces gyrating on their roots, lifting the thick moss around them. How does anything hold in this place? Without the trails it would be impossible to move. The undergrowth is a tangle of windfall, young spruce and fir, outrageous fungi, chines and crevassed rock with deep moss throats, lathered birch, aspen, broken spruce drizzling pale lichen—a fragile tumult . . .

In the end we spend two nights on the beach, slowly drain-
ing ourselves making plans to leave and trying to leave. A
strange predicament, strangely tiring: the place that enchanted
us is unquittable.

On the third morning we get up before light, eat a cold
breakfast, and send Graham and Jack off in the tandem to Terrace Bay—or whatever shore they can make—to get rescue
for Adrienne and me. The wind screams on, but the balance
between going and waiting has tilted; they will go. Adrienne
and I climb the north cliff by separate paths to watch them. It
is my Haida tableau: the women on shore with the force of their
thoughts, the men in the boats. When I'm high enough I see the
kayak, a battling little needle setting a good angle, making good
time, a red and a yellow dot paddling.

When they are out of sight I climb down to the beach and
take down my tent. If we are here tonight, I'll tent with Adrienne. We squat by the fire, find our companionship. After a
while she goes to nap and I settle myself in a pile of logs on the
west side. Little by little the day warms. I shed my parka, fleece
pants, hat. The wind drops. A couple more hours' wait and we
all could have paddled out together.

Early in the afternoon a wide motorboat comes into the bay
like the arrival of modern times. An easygoing man from town
drives the boat, Jack and Graham with him. They made Terrace Bay by strength and found Earl in his house, having coffee.
At first he declined to make the trip, but after a while he saw the
flag outside sagging and agreed to make a run.

I do not like to leave this way—by Caesarean section—but that is how we leave. I stand braced in the boat, facing backwards, the islands growing hazy, getting away, the caribou walking on their trails.

FAREWELL TO THE
NINETEENTH CENTURY

JOHN MCPHEE

John McPhee was born in Princeton, New Jersey, in 1931, attended Princeton University and, except for a single year at Cambridge, has lived in Princeton all his life. In 1965 the *New Yorker* hired him as a staff writer, and he has held that lofty position ever since. He is North America's preeminent science and nature writer, combining reporting, travel writing and the personal essay into compelling, seamless narratives. His twenty-seven books include *Coming into the Country* (1977), *Looking for a Ship* (1990), and *The Control of Nature* (1989). In 1998 his classic works on plate tectonics—*Basin and Range* (1981), *In Suspect Terrain* (1983), *Rising from the Plains* (1986), and *Assembling California* (1993)—were updated and republished, along with a fifth installment, *Crossing the Craton*, as *Annals of the Former World*, which won the 1999 Pulitzer Prize. His description of the restoration of the St. John River in Maine, reprinted here, is from *The Founding Fish* (2002), about the American shad. Since 1975 he has been Ferris Professor of Journalism at, where else, Princeton University.

• • •

WITH JOHN MCPHEDRAN, I carried a canoe around a ball-field in Waterville, Maine, and on into woods. The terrain fell away there sharply. The boat was heavy but its skin was inde-structible, and we dragged it, bumping on roots. So much for the loving care reserved for canvas, bark, and Kevlar canoes. This one had no need of it. Its makers promote its type with pic-tures that show one being thrown off the roof of their factory in Old Town. So we twitched it downhill like a log. On the thresh-old of the year 2000, this was just one of the countless ways of saying farewell to the nineteenth century.

A few days earlier, we would not have had to choose a model so tough. We put it into Messalonskee Stream, which carried us into the Kennebec River, which, in this stretch, had suddenly lost about five million tons of water as a result of deliberate demolition. Fifteen miles downstream, in Augusta, Edwards Dam, two stories high and more than nine hundred feet wide, had been breached on the first of July.

There were rapids at the mouth of Messalonskee Stream, but they had been there in pre-Columbian time. Just above the dam's impoundment, they suggested what its depth had concealed. A blue heron tried to lead us through the rapids, or seemed to, in a series of short, nosy flights down the left bank. A kingfisher watched. The Augusta Water Power Company blocked the river in the year that Martin Van Buren replaced Andrew Jackson as President of the United States. It was the year of the Panic of 1837, when real estate collapsed, banks failed like duckpins, and homeless people died in the streets. The first steam railroad was nine years old. Oberlin, the first coeducational American

college, was four years old. If you could afford Buffaloe's Oil,
you used it in your hair to fight baldness. In Augusta, primarily
thanks to the new dam, some people could afford Buffaloe's Oil.
The dam powered seven sawmills, a gristmill, and a machine
shop. Incidentally, it had a fish ladder.

Beside the second rip we came to was a sofa bed, its skirts
showing the stains of fallen water. We expected more of the
same. 'We expected grocery carts. This, after all, was not
Township 13, Range 11, of the North Woods, where nearly
half the State of Maine consists of nameless unorganized town-
ships. This was settled, supermarket Maine, but in the fifteen
river miles upstream of Augusta we would see one beer can, no
grocery carts, and three tires. Now we saw a mallard, a pewee,
goldfinches. We heard song sparrows, a wood thrush, a veery.
I wouldn't know a veery from a blue-winged warbler, but John
McPhedran is acute on birds. I had known him since he was
seventeen, seventeen years before. Since then, he had become
a botanist, a general field naturalist, and a freelance water-
quality consultant working for the Maine Department of Trans-
portation. We saw sticking up from a large and newly emergent
river boulder an iron bolt fully an inch and a half in diameter
and capped with a head like a big iron mushroom. I knew what
that dated from—the log drives of the Kennebec, which began
in colonial times and came to an end in 1976. Put a chain around
that bolt and you could stop a raft of logs.

We saw no white pines, very long gone as the masts of ships.
Or spruce, for that matter. We saw deciduous trees. In fall, the river's walls would be afire in oranges and reds, but now, in summer,

the leaves seemed too bright, too light for Maine. Among them
were few houses—in fifteen otherwise uncivilized miles, a total
of three nervous houses peeping through narrow slots in the
trees. This seemed to report a population that had turned its back
on the river, which it had, for the better part of a century, because
the river was cluttered with the debris of log drives, becessed
with community waste, spiked with industrial toxins. Square-
rigged ships once came up into the fresh Kennebec to carry its
pure ice down the east coasts of both Americas and around Cape
Horn to San Francisco, and even across the Pacific, but by the
nineteen-forties and fifties the Kennebec had developed such
a chronic reek that windows in unairconditioned offices in the
Capitol of Maine—six hundred yards from the river—were kept
tightly shut in summer. After the Clean Water Act of 1972, the
Kennebec, like so many American rivers, steadily and endur-
ingly cleared, and the scene was set for the dam destruction of
1999 and the restoration of this part of the river.

We looked down through clear water, color of pale tea, at a
variously rocky and gravelly bottom. In Maritime Canada, I had
recently fished over a scene like that in a place locally known as
the Shad Bar. Shad like to spawn over that kind of riverbed. In
this river, 1837 was not a good year for anadromous fish. Something like a million American shad came up the Kennebec before
the dam at Augusta stopped them. Immemorially, the Kenne-
becs themselves speared Atlantic salmon below falls upriver.
The fish ladder at the Augusta dam may have helped to some
extent, but it disappeared in a flood in 1838, not to be replaced.

We saw and heard three crows charily screaming at a red-tailed hawk—a sedentary drama enacted in a dying tree. A spotted sandpiper watched as well, from a newly dried rock in the fallen stream. Like a scale model of the Yukon River, the Kennebec was unfolding before us not in multiple twists and turns but in sizable segments, long reaches—a bend, a mile here, another bend, two miles there. They quickly added up to Six-Mile Falls, a rapid that was covered over by the rising impoundment in 1837, and until just a few days ago had been an engulfed series of bedrock ledges under the still-water pool. In 1826, the United States Engineer Department surveyed the Kennebec River and mapped Six-Mile Falls, so named because they were six miles downstream from Ticonic Falls, at Waterville. The engineers' report (1828) would preserve that name, if nothing else, while the surf-like sound and the roil of white water were taken away for a hundred and sixty-two years. Six-Mile Falls, the army engineers reported, were "three ledges of rock forming three distinct pitches." Downriver, we heard them now—that sound of gravel pouring on a tin drum. You don't need Sockdolager, the Upset Rapid, or Snake River Canyon to pick you up with that sound. Any riffle, let alone a small rapid, will do. I can feel adrenaline when I fill a glass of water.

Six-Mile Falls was a white riverscape of rock and plunge pools, small souse holes, tightly coiled eddies, and noisy, staired cascades. As we approached, we had to stand up and look for the thread of the river. The place was making scenery lifted from the dead. For six, seven, eight generations, it had been as withdrawn from the world as Debussy's *cathédrale engloutie*, but now, as in the time long gone, it was making its own music. Its higher rock, in broad, flat segments, was covered with filamentous algae, which under water have the look of long grass, combed straight by current. These algae were in thick brown mats, opened to the sky by the breaching of the dam and on their way to removal by the wind. We picked what seemed to be the most promising chute. The canoe slipped through it. We spun around and hung in an eddy. From riverbank to riverbank, water was falling in a hundred different ways. The truly moving fact that this scene, now restored, had been occluded for so much historic time was in an instant wiped from my mind by an even more stirring thought. Migrating fish "bag up" at the base of any rapid. You could be here during the spring migration and catch the milling shad . . .

AT ABOUT SIX AM on July 1, 1999, the first of more than a thousand spectators began to collect above the eastern end of the Augusta dam, in a place known locally as the Tree-Free Parking Lot. Tree-Free Fiber is a bankrupt company that recycled paper. The view was immediate, across three hundred yards of barrage—called Edwards Dam since the eighteen-eighties, when the Edwards Manufacturing Company bought it and was soon operating a hundred thousand spindles and employing a thousand people in one of the largest cotton mills in the world. The dam was veiled now in falling water, an exception being a gap at the west end, where sixty feet had been dismantled and removed.

A curvilinear cofferdam, convex to the current of the river, ran like a short causeway from the west shore to the broken end of the dam, cupping the wound and holding back the river.

The crowd gathered in suits, ties, and combat fatigues, sandals, sneakers, boots, and backpacks—babies in the backpacks. There were port-a-potties, T-shirts for sale, booths of brochures—Trout Unlimited, American Rivers, Salvation Army Emergency Disaster Services. There was a row of television cameras. A helicopter preëmpted the sound of the river. With "Muddy Water" and "River" and a banjo and a guitar and a pennywhistle, a trio called Schooner Fare tried to compete. Two fixed-wing planes, one of them on floats, flew in circles even tighter than the chopper's. The people had come to hear the Secretary of the Interior, the Governor of Maine, and the Mayor of Augusta—but mainly to witness the freeing of the Kennebec, the breaching of the dam...

Edwards Dam had been making electricity since 1913—lately, 3.5 megawatts, scarcely enough to light the warehouse at L.L. Bean. The license was up for renewal. Since "needed and appropriate" fishways would cost three times as much as removing the dam—and the power it produced was hardly a redeeming factor—the commission ordered the Edwards Manufacturing Company to shut down its turbines, deconstruct the dam, and restore to a natural, free-flowing state the public waterway the company had used for profit. This was the first big dam in a major river to be ordered out of existence by the federal government while the owner was left holding a wet application.

Maine's first governor (1820) was William King, a Kennebec shipbuilder, and also farmer, miller, sawyer, storekeeper, banker. A French traveller mistook him for an authentic king (according to the Kennebec poet Robert P. Tristram Coffin). In any case, King was known for being "as independent as a hog on ice." This set of facts seemed to cluster about Maine's incumbent governor—the Independent Angus King—as he rose to speak in the Tree-Free Parking Lot. He had tousled hair. He had a sandy mustache, medical in nature, and he wore a red-and-gold tie covered with blue fish. Having secured seven million dollars for the cause, he now lifted things to a loftier stratum than the lubricated trade-offs in his Kennebec River Comprehensive Hydropower Settlement Accord. Speaking without notes, he mentioned POP. He defined POP. He described the promise of its cybertronic effects in connecting entire communities to the World Wide Web, and he said that POP would be to the twenty-first century what the community dam had been to the nineteenth. It was time for the dam to go.

A year earlier, a short way downstream on the same riverbank, Bruce Babbitt, the Secretary of the Interior, had said, "This is not a call to remove all, most, or even many dams. But this is a challenge to dam owners and operators to defend themselves, to demonstrate by hard facts, not by sentiment or myth, that the continued operation of a dam is in the public interest economically and environmentally." In the months that followed, the ancestral truism "As Maine goes, so goes the nation" was frequently invoked by people proclaiming a new national momentum in sentiment toward removal of dams. And now, in an open-collar faded-brick Madras shirt, Bruce Babbitt looked across the crowd before him and counted the television cameras. He remarked on the considerable number of reporters, who had travelled from cities in four time zones. "They're not coming just to celebrate good news," he said. "I'm here to tell you, that's not what the American press is about. Reporters are here because they know this is the beginning of something that is going to affect the entire nation. It's a manifestation of who we are: neighbors living in a democracy. Before the Clean Water Act of 1972, the river was so polluted that it turned buildings black and literally peeled the paint off the walls. For healthy rivers and fisheries, the removal sets an important precedent. You're going to look back in years hence and say, 'It all began right here on this riverbank.' " Later in the day, Babbitt waxed almost Biblical, adding, "It's about coming together to restore the waters, recognizing that the rivers in turn have the power to restore our communities."

Begging his pardon, but from where I was sitting it all seemed to be about fish. Another speaker—among ten or so before and after King and Babbitt—spoke with reverence of a deceased state legislator who had helped lead the cause against the dam: "Wherever he is, I hope he's hooked to an Atlantic salmon on a fly rod somewhere," said the speaker, as if the purpose of destroying the dam was not so much to benefit as to barb fish. An economic study that might have been carried forward by a day trader had determined that forty-eight million dollars would be brought to the river by sport fishermen soon after the dam was gone. In the eighteenth century, Kennebec salmon were so abundant that farmers hiring help typically had to promise not to feed them salmon more than once a day. And now the eighteenth century—POP!—was coming back to the river.

Lewis Flagg, who was in the crowd, had told me that he expected as many as seven hundred and twenty-five thousand shad to be spawning north of Augusta in fifteen years or so. Flagg was the director of the Stock Enhancement Division of Maine's Department of Marine Resources. He enumerated the biological advantages of removing a dam—any dam. (1) It gets rid of obstructions to migration. (2) It restores natural habitat. (3) The river resumes the natural variations of its flow. (4) The siltation of spawning and feeding habitat ceases in what had been the impounded pool. (5) It gets rid of debris. (6) It gets rid of unnatural temperatures downstream. (7) It removes turbines that kill juvenile fish. Unless you're a stocked trout in the cold water downstream from a dam in Arkansas, the rationale for dam removal is quite compelling from a fish's point of view.

Schools of striped bass had been seen by construction workers nosing up to Edwards Dam that morning. A big Atlantic salmon broached and—two feet out of water—just hung there, watching. A high-school bell was mounted on a post near the microphones, and Babbitt, King, and others—on schedule with the speeches and the downstream recession of the morning tide—began to ring it. And ring it. Evan Richert, of the Maine State Planning Office, shouted into the microphones, "Set the fishery free!" He did not say, "Set free the river!"

On the cofferdam near the west bank sat Reggie Barnes, of
Alton, Maine, at the levers of a Caterpillar 345 backhoe with
a two-and-a-half-yard bucket and a thirty-nine-foot ground-
level reach. Even from across the river, it looked Cretaceous, its
head above the trees. Facing east, it swung right, and it bit a
few tons of gravel. After swinging farther to the right and dropping the load, it went back for more. It was eating the cofferdam.
It ate from south to north, toward the restrained water. Swing
left. Bite. Swing right. Drop. Swing left. Bite. The machine was
opening a chasm, and the north end of the chasm was becoming a pillar of gravel separating air from water. Bite. The pillar
thinned. Frankly, I had not imagined this moment in history to
be so dramatic—the engineering was so extensive, monumental,
and controlled. I mean, a Stuka wasn't dropping one on the crest
and flying off to Frankfurt. But this backhoe, positioned on the
very structure it was consuming—swinging to and fro on the
inboard end of the cofferdam—was hypnotizing a thousand
people. It hadn't far to go. The bucket had not reached water
before water reached the bucket. From a thousand feet away,
even through binoculars, not much could be seen yet but occasional splashes in motion, south. They were occasional enough
to cause Reggie Barnes to roll his tread and get the big backhoe
out of there, fast. It scooted off the cofferdam and partway up
a hill. A bottle of champagne had been cracked on the bucket
before it all began, and now from beneath a mass of hard hats
came a cheer that might have been audible in Portland. While
the hard hats watched and the Nature Conservancy watched
with the leaders of American Rivers, the licks and splashes

increased in frequency and height above the cofferdam, which was now being eaten by the Kennebec River.

Rapidly, it widened and deepened its advantage. It became a chocolate torrent. It shot through the gap in the western end of the dam itself and smashed into the foundation wall of the gatehouse, once the entry to the power canal. The foundation wall of the gatehouse consisted of very large blocks of granite. The liberated currents caromed off it and angled into the lower river. A milky brown plume spread through the clear water there and nearly reached the eastern shore, a thousand feet away. In eight minutes, the Kennebec, completely in charge of everything now, melted down the cofferdam until a channel had opened seventy feet wide. The rage of high water seemed to fly through the air before hitting the granite wall and exploding back into the river. In the Tree-Free Parking Lot, the assembled phalanges of the environmental movement were standing as one, standing on their chairs for a line of sight through a forest of elbows apexed with binoculars, framing Babbitt on a cell phone before the frothing river. The volume of the rapids grew. After the initial blowout of sediments, the thundering water turned white and the slicks were cordovan glass. The Kennebec River in Augusta, after hundred and sixty-two years in the slammer, was walking.

ACKNOWLEDGMENTS

"Concerning Rivers" excerpted from *The Compleat Angle*r by Izaak Walton (London: Richard Marriot, 1653).

"A Flood" excerpted from *Delineations of American Scenery and Character* by John James Audubon (New York: G.A. Baker and Company, 1926).

"My Visit to Niagara" by Nathaniel Hawthorne first published in *New-England Magazine* 8 (1835), pp. 91–96.

"The Lake of Salt" excerpted from *Journal of Researches into the Natural History and Geology of the Countries Visited During the Voyage round the World of H.M.S. Beagle under the Command of Captain Fitz Roy, R.N.* by Charles Darwin (London: Henry Colburn, 1839).

"The Tocantins and Cametá" excerpted from *The Naturalist on the River Amazons* by Henry Walter Bates (London: John Murray, 1863).

"Ganges, the Great Purifier" excerpted from *Following the Equator* by Mark Twain (New York and London: Harper and Brothers Publishers, 1890).

"The Source of the Albertine Nile" excerpted from *In Darkest Africa* by Henry Morton Stanley (New York: Charles Scribner's Sons, 1890).

"Speckled Trout" excerpted from *The Writings of John Burroughs: Locusts and Wild Honey* by John Burroughs (Boston and New York: Houghton Mifflin Company, 1903).

"Lake Ontario" excerpted from *Letters from America* by Rupert Brooke (London: Sidgwick and Jackson, 1916, 1947, and 2002).

"The Thames" excerpted from *A Traveler at Forty* by Theodore Dreiser (New York: The Century Co., 1913).

"The St. Lawrence" excerpted from *The St. Lawrence* by Henry Beston, published in the Rivers of America series (New York and Toronto: Farrar and Rinehart Inc., 1942).

"Falling Water" excerpted from *The Road of a Naturalist* by Donald Culross Peattie. Copyright © 1941 by Donald Culross Peattie, © renewed 1969 by Louise Redfield Peattie. Reprinted by permission of Houghton Mifflin Company. All rights reserved.

"The Fraser" excerpted from *The Fraser* by Bruce Hutchison (New York: Holt, Rinehart and Winston, 1950).

"The Big Blackfoot" excerpted from *A River Runs Through It* by Norman Maclean (Chicago: University of Chicago Press, 1976). Reprinted by permission of University of Chicago Press.

"Awash in the Baleh" excerpted from *Into the Heart of Borneo* by Redmond O'Hanlon (Edinburgh: Salamander Press, 1984). Reprinted by permission of SLL/Sterling Lord Literistic, Inc. Copyright by Francis Russell.

"The River" excerpted from *Measure of the Year* by Roderick Haig-Brown (Toronto and London: Collins, 1950).

"The Hawkesbury" is excerpted from *The Secret River* by Kate Grenville (Edinburgh: Canongate Books/New York: Grove/Atlantic, Inc., 2005). Copyright © 2005 by Kate Grenville. Used by permission of Grove/ Atlantic, Inc.

"We Start up the Great Missouri" excerpted from *River-Horse: Across America by Boat* by William Least Heat-Moon. Copyright © 1999 by William Least Heat-Moon. Reprinted by permission of Houghton Mifflin Company. All rights reserved.

"The Tree and the Trout" is extracted from the book *Coming West: A Natural History of Home* by Kevin Van Tighem, published by Altitude Publishing, Canmore, Alberta, and is reprinted with the permission of the author.

"Adoration of a Hose" is excerpted from *My Story As Told by Water* by David James Duncan (San Francisco: Sierra Club Books, 2001).

"Bank Deposits" excerpted from *River in a Dry Land: A Prairie Passage* by Trevor Herriot © 2000. Published by McClelland and Stewart Ltd. Used with permission of the publisher.

"Superior" excerpted from *Starting Out in the Afternoon: A Mid-Life Journey into the Wild Land* by Jill Frayne. Copyright © 2002 Jill Frayne. Reprinted by permission of Random House Canada.

"Farewell to the Nineteenth Century" excerpted from *The Founding Fish* by John McPhee (New York: Farrar, Straus and Giroux, 2002).

Northern Wild by David R. Boyd, ed.

Greenhouse by Gale E. Christianson

Vanishing Halo by Daniel Gawthrop

The Sacred Balance: Rediscovering Our Place in Nature
by David Suzuki and Amanda McConnell

Dead Reckoning by Terry Glavin

Delgamuukw by Stan Persky

The Plundered Seas by Michael Berrill

DAVID SUZUKI FOUNDATION CHILDREN'S TITLES

Salmon Forest by David Suzuki and Sarah Ellis;
illustrated by Sheena Lott

You Are the Earth by David Suzuki and Kathy Vanderlinden

Eco-Fun by David Suzuki and Kathy Vanderlinden

The David Suzuki Foundation works through science and education to protect the diversity of nature and our quality of life, now and for the future.

With a goal of achieving sustainability within a generation, the Foundation collaborates with scientists, business and industry, academia, government and non-governmental organizations. We seek the best research to provide innovative solutions that will help build a clean, competitive economy that does not threaten the natural services that support all life.

The Foundation is a federally registered independent charity, which is supported with the help of over 50,000 individual donors across Canada and around the world.

We invite you to become a member. For more information on how you can support our work, please contact us:

The David Suzuki Foundation
219–2211 West 4th Avenue
Vancouver, BC
Canada v6k 4s2
www.davidsuzuki.org
contact@davidsuzuki.org
Tel: 604-732-4228 · Fax: 604-732-0752

Checks can be made payable to The David Suzuki Foundation. All donations are tax-deductible.
Canadian charitable registration: (BN) 12775 6716 rr0001
U.S. charitable registration: #94-3204049